CASH FLOW
NOW

How To Create Multiple Streams
of Real Estate Income

JIM INGERSOLL

**Praise for Jim Ingersoll's *Cash Flow Now:*
*How To Create Multiple Streams of Real Estate Income***

"*Cash Flow Now* offers a simple but powerful approach to generating real estate cash flow in today's market. Author Jim Ingersoll does a great job showing how anyone can generate monthly cash flow from today's real estate opportunities. I'll be strongly recommending *Cash Flow Now* to our 70,000 Newsletter subscribers."

J.P. Vaughan, J.D.
Publisher, Creative Real Estate Online
www.creonline.com

"Today's market is all about cash flow and Jim Ingersoll's terrific book, *Cash Flow Now*, hits the high points very well. This is a must read book."

Eddie Speed, Founder of Note School

"The Dallas Mavericks owner is famous for his business advice and said, "sales cure all." Another way to say it is "Cash Flow Cures All." If you don't have cash flow, you have stress. This book is a must read for anyone looking to plan for the future and enjoy life more."

Ron White - 2 Time USA Memory Champion -
www.BrainAthlete.com

"Cash flow is the life blood of any business. Simply put, generating a healthy cash flow from your real estate investments not only allows you to quit your job, it also allows you the ability to live an enviable lifestyle. Jim Ingersoll does a wonderful job of showing you how you can do this for yourself and your family. A must read for every real estate investor or anybody contemplating getting into this fascinating and very profitable field."

Scott Britton, Founder of *"Creative Real Estate Solutions"*
www.scottbritton.com

"Cash is king and Jim Ingersoll is king of teaching cash flow. This is a must read for both experienced and inexperienced investors. His book is a gold mine of gold nuggets. In the explanation of income streams, Jim not only defines the different possibilities for income streams but explains the opportunities and processes as well. This is a highly recommended book for any investor."

Selina Stoller: www.MyREIadvisor.com

"Jim is one of the few people who's writing I can trust. *Cash Flow Now* will show you how to grow and thrive while others are cowering, retreating and running away."

Michael Jake, Founder of Swift Results, Inc

"*Cash Flow Now* will prepare you to gain control over uncertainty at a time when many others are busy burying their head in the sand. This book is a roadmap that allows readers to control their own destiny."

David Phelps, Founder David Phelps International

"Jim's new book *Cash Flow Now* really nails it. Jim does a superb job explaining how to create multiple streams of income. If you want freedom in your life, this is the book to read."

Damon Janis, Founder of Insider's Circle at Lifestyles Unlimited
www.luinsiderscircle.com

"Jim Ingersoll does a great job providing some alternate investment strategies that go beyond the typical stocks, bonds and mutual funds using self-directed IRA's and Joint Ventures. These methods can set provide you with plenty of cash flow for your retirement years."

David Huber
www.ira.com and www.stockmarkettoday.com

"Wow!! I wish this had been my first real estate invest-ing book! Not only does it give you down to earth useful advice, but it motivates you to get started... right now! Most of the books I've read about real estate bog you down with information you will never use. Jim Ingersoll's book is easy to read and understand. Truly a great book that will get you to shift your gears to obtain cash flow from real estate."

Troy Ross, Founder and President RREIA

CreateSpace, North Charleston, SC

This publication is designed to provide accurate and authoritative information in regard to the subject matter covered. It is sold with the understanding that neither the author nor publisher is engaged in rendering legal, accounting, or other professional service. If legal advice or other expert assistance is required, the services of a competent professional should be sought.

ISBN: 1470118467
ISBN-13: 9781470118464

Dedication

This book is dedicated to everyone seeking additional cash flow in today's challenging economy.

Thank you to my parents who helped me understand the value of a strong work ethic along with providing a path that led to investing in real estate.

A **special** thank you to my best friend and wife. Cheryl you continue to be my inspiration! To the two best daughters a father could ever have, Melisa and Carisa you are amazing, and I am glad you are both investing in real estate at a young age. Finally, Luke, welcome to our family!

Acknowledgements

Thank you to my good friend and colleague, David Phelps. Cheryl and I love working with you and Kandace and appreciate you both very much.

Thank you to Scott Britton, Walter Wofford, Quincy Long, and John Groom. I appreciate the collaboration!

Thank you to those who continue to help me spread the message of *Cash Flow Now and Investing Now* on each of their websites.

Damon Janis -- www.lifestylesunlimited.com
JP Vaughn – www.Creonline.com
David Huber – www.ira.com
Selina Stoller – www.myREIadvisor.com

A special shout of thanks to Michael Jake who continues to crush it in Colorado!

To everyone local on my Richmond, VA team helping us buy, renovate, sell, and rent houses—THANK YOU!

This includes: Mark J, Traci, Jose, Linda, Brad, Enrique, Andre, Mike W, Vicki, Mike N, Charlotte, Julie, Doug, Andy, Scott, Mark D, Steven, Harvey B, Keith and so many more!!!

Contents

FOREWORD

At the time of the publishing of this book, our nation, in conjunction with the global economy, is wrestling with the consequences of long-standing socialistic policies and fiat spending, primarily into entitlement programs which have driven the welfare states of these countries into debt that cannot be maintained. This is an entirely new era for which the majority living today have no historical precedent, no experience and no idea of how to adjust, accommodate, and most importantly, protect themselves from the likelihood of stark changes in lifestyle and freedom of choice that have been enjoyed by Americans for many generations.

What this means to each of us is that we either take control of what we can control or we adopt a policy of "things are surely going to get better."

For those who take the latter stance, I have no advice. Good luck. For those who wish to be proactive, this book, *Cash Flow Now*, can provide a solid basis for taking appropriate action.

The old model of "earning one's way to retirement" through savings and profit sharing plans as a company or corporate employee is no longer viable. In addition, due to the massive debt compilation by our country's administrations and politicians, we face a future of rising interest rates, hyperinflation and a decreasing standard of living. More and more people will become dependent on the government for a very meager or basic subsistence.

The opportunity that the economic turbulence and chaos creates, is the first imperative of the person who seeks to maintain independence. Once that opportunity is defined, action is the next step. Finally, speed to the desired goal can be obtained in one of two ways; by trial and error or by following in the footsteps of other thought leaders. Either method may work, however, the amount of time available must be considered before making a decision. Currently, our country appears to be on a fast track to becoming another Greece. Let your own observations be your guide.

Financial security, before anything else is of paramount importance. Cash flow, when secured by a hard asset, is the basis for creating multiple streams of diversified income which leads to security, options and finally, freedom.

Real estate has historically created more wealth than any other investment platform. This exchange or transfer of wealth has happened over and over again and most clearly during times of recession or depression. Understanding the dynamics at play in the current market and how to position one to leverage the voids in the market with low downside risk is the key to profits and wealth.

Jim Ingersoll is an author and information leader in the real estate industry. He is first and foremost a doer. He made the decision a number of years ago to take back his life and not be dependent on a company or corporation for his livelihood. He moved from a professional career as an engineer to real estate entrepreneur. He made this successful transition during one of the worst credit and housing downfalls in our country's history.

This is not a one-size-fits-all treatise. The reader of this book should be able to come away with a new perspective into how to create safety and security for a much unknown future. He or she will understand the key concepts in true real estate wealth creation and which investment format works best for his or her own retirement plan portfolio.

The key to one's future is to take specific action now. Don't be caught looking back in five or ten years and wonder what happened, and more importantly, why there was a failure to act. The time is now.

To your freedom,
David Phelps, D.D.S.
www.DavidPhelpsInternational.com

David Phelps began investing in real estate while still in dental school in 1980. His first joint venture partner was his father, whom David convinced to be the financial partner in a rental property that David managed during professional training at Baylor College of Dentistry in Dallas. After graduating dental school in 1983, he never looked back and began a steady and continuous progression in real estate education and investment for the remainder of his practice career. "Creating multiple streams of income that would provide for me and my family, in an emergency, for college tuition, and for retirement, was always a primary goal."

Freedom is his mantra; he is a crusader for dentists, small business and professional practice owners, to achieve the same life that he has engineered. Real estate continues to be his passion as a proven investment vehicle over many years and economic cycles, a subject on which David mentors other enterprising individuals.

WHY CASH FLOW NOW?

Can you believe all the negative news we are bombarded with on a daily basis? Between terrorism, governments being overthrown, political division, and the constant economic challenges you may be wondering how I could publish a book titled *Cash Flow Now*.

How could a book called *Cash Flow Now* make any sense with today's high unemployment, Wall Street greed, a tanking stock market, and a government that spends way more than it takes in?

With a housing market that collapsed in 2008 when the bubble burst, upside down houses, and nothing but bad housing news day in and day out, how can you make sense of this market and create income streams today? The good news is that these exact economic, social, and political challenges have created tremendous new opportunities for those willing to venture out and invest today.

OK, let me make a confession. I am an eternal optimist and I know it. My father-in-law, Doug Johnson, and I debate on this subject on a regular basis. He considers himself a "realist" and I tell him he is realistically a pessimist with his glass half empty. I am an optimist partly because the people I surround myself with are mostly optimists. That list starts with my own father. He has always been very positive, no matter what challenges and circumstances he faces. My father had to make an adjustment at a very young age when he lost his own father to cancer. He was then thrown into helping hold his own family together and providing financial support when he was just 16 years old. All through his life he has had an optimistic outlook on every challenge that he faced. My wife Cheryl, is another optimist in my life. She provides me with support and knows how to handle the peaks and valleys of life while remaining positive and keeping our family on track. These are the types of people who have shaped my belief that every challenge is a new opportunity.

These days, we are all experiencing peaks and valleys as we are bombarded with so much negative news every single day of our lives. You can watch mainstream news, read the magazines, or check out the headlines on the front page of your local newspaper to see exactly what I mean.

Since 2008 we have been experiencing a very serious economic downturn that has included high unemployment, a burst housing bubble, and a stock market that continues to lose.

We all realize we are in the worst economic downturn since the 1930s. The media selectively distorts the issues and the politicians are playing party politics stronger than at any time in our lifetimes. Below is the unemployment rate since 1965. You can see the spike in unemployment that our nation has been wrestling with the past few years.

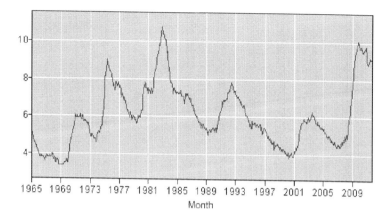

This is a book about creating multiple income streams using real estate as a vehicle to make it happen. Housing reports forecast a down market for the foreseeable future and shadow foreclosure inventory remains high. Ultimately, the housing market cannot fully recover until our economy strengthens and the unemployment rate improves significantly. We all have money challenges of some sort with today's economy. I will cover that in detail in the next chapter.

What does this mean for you? You have two options to consider while reading this book.

Either you take no action; put your head in the sand and hope and pray for everything to go back to 'the good old days' before 2008, or you prepare to take action now; you realize that we live in a completely different world economy today and that definitive action is necessary in order to survive and maintain the lifestyle and retirement you deserve.

Inaction in today's world could very possibly result in financial disaster. The good news is that strategic action taken now can make positive changes in the lives of those who are informed – positive changes of a magnitude that will surpass investment opportunities or strategies of the past. Now is the time to learn to capitalize in real estate with multiple income streams to get your finances back on track.

It is interesting how two very different perspectives and approaches can produce such drastically different outcomes.

No one has a magic crystal ball, but history will show that those who act based on a solid strategy with well-defined criteria and a systematic approach will be the very people who make tremendous amounts of money when everyone else is paralyzed with confusion and inaction.

"Buy when there is blood in the streets." was the famous saying attributed to financier Baron Rothschild during the 1871 panic sell-off in London. Baron Rothschild was a successful financier from a banking family who was prepared to take definitive action following the battle of Waterloo. Rothschild's strategy was to use advanced "inside" information regarding the battle's outcome and large scale market manipulation to take advantage of a chaotic situation and make large investment gains. He succeeded.

Billions and trillions of dollars will change hands during this economic down cycle and I expect that we will experience the greatest transfer of real estate wealth of our generation. The question is will all these negative indicators and the bad news make you freeze or will you be prepared to add income streams and assets to set you free?

This is the "why" behind this book. People today feel trapped, betrayed, and frozen and I want to show you methods and plans that will enable you to feel liberated to take control of your personal financial future. I realize this is contrarian to the recent actions of our politicians who want to provide bailouts and freebies to everyone. I want to show you several different income streams that can help you pay down personal debt, get your children through college, and prepare you for retirement.

My wife Cheryl and I bought our first income investment property when we were 25, in 1990. We had no training on investment real estate, no clue how to fix it up and no ideas how to manage the property. Even though we were in way over our heads back in 1990; it all turned out fine in the end because real estate can be quite forgiving. We learned a lot from this very first investment property and I will share the entire story in chapter 6 of this book. Since then we have bought and sold hundreds of houses while building a portfolio of rental properties that provide monthly cash flow. Below is a photo of the first duplex investment property we purchased in Jamestown, NY.

This is the absolute best market for buying houses that my wife and I have experienced and I hear the same from many long-term investors who have been investing in real estate for decades. The new real estate market we are experiencing now makes it easier than ever to create multiple streams of income to meet your financial goals.

Help is exactly what families need these days, but the help does not need to come in the form of more government bailouts and entitlement programs. I want to stimulate your mind, help you to develop the income streams you need to make it happen and encourage you to have the confidence to make it happen this year.

What is the number one thing holding you back from moving forward? Are you paralyzed with FEAR? Maybe you are stuck in the national credit crunch or have bruised credit. Maybe you don't know how to move forward because you don't have cash on hand to invest. Perhaps you are experiencing the pain of watching your 401k and other retirement investment continue to drop.

The good news is that by reading this book you are investing in yourself by learning some great ways to produce cash flow by leveraging real estate. Investing in yourself will help break down the FEAR barrier as you begin to understand how to put deals together and create income streams. I will also help you understand that you can buy real estate without needing a bank mortgage, great credit, or cash in your checking account. Finally I look forward to your reading the chapter "Future Cash Flow: Great returns for retirement." This is one of my favorite chapters of the book where I unveil one of the best-kept secrets in America, which is the power of a Roth Self Directed IRA. I look forward to showing you ways to make huge returns and then draw the funds out tax-free in your Roth IRA.

Buy when there's blood in the streets much like Baron Rothschild did after Waterloo. It sounds easy enough, but what are the options and what is the best way to start? I am happy to show you how to create transactions that provide you with income streams now. You will find a number of different income streams in this book and many of them will show you how to structure joint ventures where multiple people can profit in the same real estate deal.

This is the essence of why it is so important and relevant to families today. The entire process begins with a sharp paradigm shift in your thinking. How can you retrain your brain to be positive and ready for action when the media and everyone else is so negative.

For me it came naturally from my father being so positive in all circumstances. For you it may be more challenging, as you may be unemployed, facing a foreclosure, or just going through a rough time in your life. If you are not optimistic now, you need to take a careful look at how you can turn your mindset around from the negative to the positive. Being a realist is not good enough; you need to retrain your brain to look at challenges as opportunities. For me, this starts with my faith in God and knowing beyond any shadow of doubt that God has a purpose and path for my life. Part of my purpose includes reaching out to help others, which is one reason I love to write books.

When I had a corporate job I use to travel internationally all the time and I enjoyed seeing the world. I quickly got tired of all the trips to third world countries helping to open factories and move our jobs off shore. I was travelling continually for about 10 years of my corporate career. When we moved from New York to Virginia I was in Mexico when my wife bought our home, then I was in England when our furniture arrived and a month later I was sent to China. Prior to moving from New York I was travelling regularly to Europe. One night I woke up in a hotel in Germany and didn't even remember where I was. You can see why I got tired of climbing the corporate ladder and eventually jumped off.

Now when I travel internationally it will only be for a family vacation, a trip to invest in myself for some training and networking, or a trip with a purpose to help others.

One of my favorite recent trips was to Sao Paulo, Brazil where I worked at the Seeds of Hope trade school which is designed to provide skills to orphans when they are kicked out of the orphanage. I love the fulfillment that is realized reaching out to a third world country, rather than just doing business in a third world country. Below is a photo of me when I was in Sao Paulo. I highly recommend you find a great organization, such as Seeds of Hope, and help find your purpose.

You may need to start by examining your own purpose and faith as well as looking at the people you are closely associating with. Are you connecting with mostly negative people or mostly positive minded people? The power of a positive attitude is contagious and you will improve your own attitude if you begin to associate with more positive people in your life. Work specifically on removing words and phrases from your speech such as "can't", "won't work," "fail" and "lose." I know the TV show "Biggest Loser" is very popular but I would love to see a show created called "Biggest Winner" featuring contestants getting their financial world in order. In fact, you might consider disconnecting your TV entirely. Use the Internet for your news and information. Internet news comes from a much more diverse and trustworthy set of sources and there is instant information for any subject you can imagine. You will be able to select your own subjects, times for viewing, and sources that you trust.

Also, what are you listening to on your play list these days? Are you listening to music and podcasts that pull you down or lift you up? Try listening to songs like "We Are the Champions," "I Gotta A Feeling", and other uplifting songs. I use my iPhone to provide me with a lot of music and other positive content while working out, driving, etc. I find it to be a great opportunity to listen to great speakers and uplifting songs on a regular basis.

A change in mindset starts with the small steps such as connecting with the right people, listening to the right music, reading the right books, and investing in yourself to help you shift your attitude. Give it a try today and you will enjoy attracting positive and like-minded individuals who will share your positive outlook.

Growing up in Jamestown, NY our family was taught to work hard; I mean really work hard every single day. My father was the quintessential hard working, always providing father. For him it started when he was just 16 and his own father died unexpectedly. He had brothers and sisters who needed to be fed and a farm to attend to. That was the start of a life of a hard work ethic for my father. Growing up there was never a doubt from anyone in my family that my dad was always working hard, never complaining, and always providing. That transferred directly to my brothers and I.

All three of us had entrepreneurial tendencies and a hard work ethic which allowed us to learn about cash flow at an early age. My brother Bill started the ball rolling selling seeds door to door when he was about nine years old and then graduated to a paper route. Not just a normal paper route though; Bill found a way purchase two separate paper routes and combine them without telling the Jamestown Post Journal. He paid $15 for one of those routes and ended up with 148-house paper route. When he was in his early teens he "sold" his paper routes to the next genera-tion of enterprising young people and moved onto "trap-ping." Only Bill could find a way to turn a hobby into a cash flow stream before he was 15 years old. He always loved being outdoors and was always hunting, fishing and trap-ping. He would set traps and then go check them before he went to school each day. He would get $2 for muskrat, $15 for coon and $40 if he was lucky to get a fox. To this day he loves being outdoors and is the ultimate fly fisherman.

My brother David was the same way, all three of us brothers had paper routes and started working in our early teens. David took his collectible hobbies and created cash flow by buying and selling sports memorabilia, coins, toys, and even pez dispensers. To this day, he continues to enjoy creating cash flow by buying and selling collectibles. He buys large collections on Craigslist, breaks them into smaller pieces and resells them right on eBay. He and his wife Tracy have a busy collectible internet business that helps them with extra cash flow each month.

Cash flow is a term used to describe the movement of money. Growing up my brothers and I always found ways to create cash flow, even at a young age. Money is always flowing as you earn it from investments or working a job and as you spend it on everything from groceries to entertainment and toys. The question to answer is whether your current situation has a positive or negative cash flow. If you are spending more than you are earning then you have negative cash flow. In today's economy millions of folks are experiencing negative cash flow. Their negative cash flow can result from job loss, declining retirement funds, or an increase in living expenses.

There are quite a few books available that deal with reducing expenses and helping people get out of debt. One of my favorite authors who teachs this principal is Dave Ramsey. Families get in over their heads with excess spending and the weight of that debt becomes insurmountable for many people. Dave Ramsey said it best when he uttered this quote "Debt is Dumb. Cash is king." Susie Orman also put debt in perspective when she said, "If you have debt I'm willing to bet that general clutter is a problem for you too." The point is that if you continue to accumulate things you don't really need and spend money you don't really have you will experience negative cash flow. When you do that you will begin to have a lot of bad debt. There are two solutions for improving your cash flow in life or business. You can cut spending and live on what you earn or you can increase your earnings. Authors such as Dave Ramsey and Susie Orman both do a great job coaching people on living within their means. This book, *Cash Flow Now* is all about coaching readers on how to improve their cash flow right now.

The question you need to ask yourself is how much income do you need and how fast do you need to increase it. Some people need income to get credit cards and cars paid off. Others are looking to save for their kids college tuition or a wedding. Still others are looking for ways to increase their income once they retire. As you explore the multiple streams of income presented in this book please consider what you plan to do with your extra income streams and how fast you need to accelerate your cash flow. The answer to these questions will help lead you to the right income streams for your situation.

The income streams presented are broken into two major sections. The first is active income streams. I use the word active because they take active participation in order to be successful. Each of them can be pursued either part-time or can lead you into a full-time business model. The other income streams presented are the passive streams. The passive streams require far less work. Instead, you will learn how to make your money work for you by pursuing assets and building wealth for the long-term.

CHAPTER 1 SUMMARY

1. What is your motivation for adding a new income stream? Mine was so that I could escape the corporate life and spend more time with my family. What is your reason for wanting more income now?

2. What is the number one thing that continues to hold you back from getting started? Many people are afraid because of the media's negative news, others do not know how to get started. How about you?

3. Do you need a mind-shift from being negative to becoming positive? If so, how will you make the transition? For me it started with surrounding myself with positive people. Do you realize that on average your income level matches the ten people you are around the most? Who are those ten people for you? Are they positive or negative?

4. What is the number one thing holding you back?

Chapter 2

EVERYONE HAS A MONEY PROBLEM

You may be wondering how I could go from encouraging you to become the ultimate positive thinker right into a chapter about everyone having a money problem. If so, I am glad you are engaging your brain in the process. Now stay with me here because the truth is that this economy is so bad that virtually everyone has a money problem. You may be thinking that your money problems are worse than everyone else's or you may be thinking you have minimal money problems, but either way I think you will enjoy this segment of the book.

Let me start with the obvious group who has very serious money problems. Millions of people have lost their jobs since 2008. Since that time many people have lost their unemployment benefits and many still do not have a job. If you want to understand the magnitude of having no job for a couple years spend a moment and consider what it would be like to have virtually no income to live on. The unemployment problems we are experiencing are serious. Additionally, if you have not lost your job, you are most likely doing more work than you use to and you may not have received a pay raise in recent years. Unemployment also leads to long-term loss of retirement preparedness as many families with a 401k have had to reach into that retirement account just to survive and there are no employee or employer contributions while unemployed.

There is also a non-financial impact created with prolonged unemployment in the area declining self-esteem and loss of confidence. On top of the psychological effects of serious financial problems comes the rise in foreclosures, crime, and even homelessness. The magnitude of prolonged unemployment on a person's life cannot be overstated as it has financial, psychological, and social impacts. If you fall into this category of money problems then I am very glad you are reading this book. You will find ways to create income without needing a government bailout or a new entitlement program. You will find several different ways to add income and wealth to your life. Review the methods presented and resolve to make one of them work for you.

Maybe you are not one of the millions of people who have lost a job or lost a house, but you likely still have some concerns about your finances. This economy has impacted everyone, including those with plenty of wealth. You may be wondering how can someone with substantial financial resources be impacted by the downturn in our economy, but let me assure you that millions of people with plenty of resources are also experiencing a different level of money problems.

If you are a member of middle class America, you too have experienced some money problems though your problems are somewhere in between those who have lost jobs and the affluent. If you are in middle America you are likely experiencing the crunch of higher gas prices, rising tuition, rising food prices, and the impact of the a tough housing market. The house you are living in may be worth less than what you owe and you are no longer able to do an annual refinance to pay down the annual spending binge on your credit cards. You have likely pulled back on savings for your children's college and your own retirement.

The money problems of the affluent do certainly differ from the money problems of the unemployed, but they have their problems nonetheless. Even celebrities with million dollar incomes have their share of financial challenges along the way. Generally they somehow spend more than they make or make some poor investment choices by listening to the wrong people. Others make other poor life decisions that cost them many millions of dollars. One well known case is that of Tiger Woods who lost millions in endorsements and then lost even more when he went through his divorce.

The US government is also experiencing serious money problems. The first three words of our constitution are "We the people" but our government has become overgrown and continues to spend more than it takes in. This is the formula for financial disaster. No one, especially our government, should spend more than they make. When people spend more than they make they end up owing a lot of money to credit card companies, but, unfortunately in the case of our government our credit card company is in the form of another country named China.

I want to highlight that everyone does have a money problem, whether you feel dirt poor right now, are sitting in middle class America, a celebrity, or even part of the wealthiest class.

When developing the mindset for multiple streams of real estate income it is important to understand how to solve money problems for people and create win-win real estate transactions. One of the biggest obstacles to overcome is real estate funding because houses are still big ticket items, even though they are sometimes cheaper than buying a new car. If you can better understand how to joint venture and help people achieve tremendous returns using real estate you will find great success in creating income streams.

What kind of money problems can you solve using real estate? Let's start with asset protection, the problems millions of people are having trying to find a safe way to hold onto their money.

The poor performance of the stock market has hurt a lot of people over the past several years. It has hurt personal investment accounts along with plenty of 401k and retirement accounts. The Dow was created in 1896 and it represented the average of 12 stocks. Since its introduction in 1896 it has been modified several times into today's components, which are 30 different companies. The only company that has been on the Dow since it started in 1896 is General Electric. The Dow is one major index that represents the performance of the stock market.

The stock market has a history of sharp drops such as the crash of 1929 which led into the great depression, and others include "black Monday" in 1987 and the 9-11 attacks in 2001. But even in 2011 the market was extremely challenged. Some of the recent market news has included the following headlines.

"Fear drives perfect storm of selling"
"Dow drops over 500 points, 9th largest drop…"
"Stocks down 10% in just 10 days"
"U.S. loses top credit rating"

The domestic issues that have resulted from out-of-control US government spending and economic issues in European countries like Italy and Greece have further challenged the stock market's stability.

Today the Dow Jones is hovering in the 13,000 range and my point is that it was also in this same range of value several different times since 1999. In November, 2011 the market dropped 6% in just 30 days. People with money in the stock market have serious money problem. They struggle with what to do with their accounts, do they pull the money out now and take the loss at the end of the year or do they leave it in the market hoping to regain a portion of their loss. The challenge is that it is very hard to make up for the loss because the market has to have a huge rally to get you back to break even and start to produce any sort of positive return on investment.

If you are very wealthy and have $5M invested in the 30 stocks that comprise the Dow Jones Industrial Average, you would have lost $300,000 on 1 November 2011 if you sell the stock. If you don't sell the stock you are gambling future losses and trying to determine how big of a market rally you really need to regain your $300,000 of losses in November 2011. Many well off people are likely losing sleep as their stock market investments are dropping quickly and they don't know what to do with their money. That is why the wealthy are also having money problems.

If the money is taken out of the market where can you put it where it is safe and secure and maybe earn a reasonable return? For many people the answer to this question was to move their funds into bank CD's. At least the funds will be secure up to the FDIC of $250,000 per depositor and they cut off the losses from the stock market. But, can they handle the prospect of having nearly no returns on all that capital? A CD sounds like a safe and secure investment, but the safety and security will cost a lot in the way of virtually no returns on investment.

In December 2011 CD rates are not providing much return on investment. If you have $100,000 to invest you can earn between .5% and 2.0% if you are able to invest in the CD for one to five years. Generally the longer the term and higher the balance will lead to a slightly higher return. But also remember that if you want to use the invested capital before the term expires you generally have to pay penalties and will lose most of your interest. The CD rates generally provide a return that is near the anticipated inflation rate so the owner of the CD is safe and secure by FDIC but in reality is not earning much of a return.

People who have moved funds from the stock market into a CD certainly have money problems. If you have moved $100,000 from the stock market and placed it into a three year CD earning 1.5%, how much money will you have when the three-year term expires? Exactly $104,568. The $4,568 in interest will not keep up with inflation.

This is what is happening in today's economic climate, balances are not growing any faster than the inflation rate. Millions of dollars are moving out of the stock market and investors are looking for new alternate ways to earn a reasonable rate on their investment so they can get their plans for retirement, college savings, and so on back on track.

Everyone does have a money problem. The money problems today are debilitating at the lower income levels, but do extend to middle class America, our own government, and to the wealthiest people in our nation.

The real question is simply how can we solve these problems with alternate investments and get our lives' back on track to meeting our financial goals. Real estate is still a big-ticket item and houses still cost a lot of money. I want to show you how to solve money problems and develop funding streams that allow you to buy houses without needing cash or a typical bank mortgage. I am glad you are tracking with me on this subject as I have a lot of content ahead in this book that will help you understand how to solve the problems using real estate as the vehicle to make it happen today.

CHAPTER 2 SUMMARY

1. Can you see how everyone has a money problem? I hope you feel better about your personal situation now. What is your biggest money challenge?

2. The wealthy and top earners have money problems. If you had $5M in the market in November 2011 and had to absorb the 6% loss it provided, how much did you lose in one month?

3. The middle class has money problems. How are the 401k accounts doing these days? If you move $100k into a CD and earn 1.5% for three years, how much do you have at the end of the three year term? Are you satisfied with that return?

4. Folks in the lower income brackets are definitely struggling in this economy. What are some of their challenges?

5. Who can you think of that could benefit from solving money problems? Write their names here and consider giving them a copy of this book.

Buying Foreclosures and Distressed Houses

All of the income streams in this book are predicated on your ability to understand that real estate is on-sale and distressed houses are more readily available to buy today than any time in recent history. The vast majority of the distressed housing opportunities are being made available from foreclosures and short sales, but there are also other opportunities to buy houses that are not even listed for sale with a realtor. I want to start with understanding the foreclosure opportunity that exists in today's market.

What was it that helped create this huge opportunity to buy houses far below what they are actually worth? The greed associated with the sale of mortgages led to loose credit and the new industry of sub-prime mortgages was created in the early 21st century. The mortgage lending industry had unlimited funding available as a result of Fannie Mae, Freddie Mac and others wanting to originate and then sell as many mortgages as possible. This greed then spiraled into a new breed of mortgages being offered that included no documentation loans that would qualify borrowers based on their own stated income levels. On top of the no-documentation requirements and stated income the mortgage industry began to allow 100% financing and simultaneously lowered credit score requirements for borrowers. Essentially borrowers could buy houses with no money down, no income to support the payments, and poor credit.

This helped lead the charge of many people buying homes that they could not afford which resulted in hyper demand of houses and a surge in prices and appreciation in many markets across America. Those were the days when houses sold super fast regardless of condition and often times the best homes would receive multiple offers. Realtor's began to exploit the use of escalation clauses on their offers on a regular basis.

These toxic loans helped to over-inflate the housing market with extreme appreciation in cities such as Las Vegas, Phoenix, and throughout Florida. As the credit situation began to unravel and credit started to tighten with the reduction in mortgages being originated the value of Fannie Mae, Freddie Mac and others began to plummet. The leaders of these organizations attempted to assure the public that they would get everything back on track; but obviously that did not happen. The housing market bubble began to pop, values on Wall Street began to plummet and unemployment began to increase.

It is the combination of these and many other factors that created the opportunities of today. It is at the expense of jobs, lost value on the stock market, lost value of housing, and more importantly the lost opportunity of home ownership as banks began foreclosing on the very mortgages they should have never originated in the first place.

Financial institutions quickly learned what was involved with a non-performing asset as they displaced millions of people out of their homes and put those homes onto their own balance sheets. It started with the greed of bankers wanting to originate as many mortgages as possible, eliminating borrower qualifications and putting homeowners into homes they could not afford. It has resulted in a burst housing bubble, lower housing prices, tight credit guidelines of today, and many great people losing their homes. Everyone has personal friends who lost their homes during this crisis and my heart goes out to them. It is a tragedy that started with the greed of needing to originate loans and reducing borrower qualifications.

These toxic loans helped create an unprecedented level of distressed property inventory. Many homeowners losing their homes give up on adding value to the property and general maintenance. They were in homes they could not afford and some of them could not keep up with leaky roofs, blown heat pumps and a myriad of other challenges that come with home ownership. Many also intentionally damaged their homes with holes in the walls and general property damage. I have seen some cases of direct vandalism of their own homes including taking the heat pump with them and drilling holes into galvanized piping and a host of other items. I suspect that the foreclosing banks drove these homeowners crazy during the foreclosure process to the point that they intentionally vandalized their own homes right before they were forced out of their house.

Financial institutions quickly discovered that taking back a foreclosure was an expensive event. Besides all the legal fees, they discovered the cost of maintaining vacant property is also expensive. They learned about all the additional fees from asset management companies, vacant property insurance, costs to secure property and in some cases make the home safe, utilities, realtor commission fee's when they go to sell the house, and so on. Their expenses associated with holding non-performing assets from foreclosures are very high. This is why financial institutions that hold foreclosures in inventory are motivated sellers.

One of the first keys to real estate income streams is to realize that you make the most money when you buy; not from property upgrades and value added renovations. The good news is that there is a lot of real estate available due to the high level of foreclosures. The foreclosure inventory makes it much easier to find great deals on houses priced far below what they are worth. In the next few chapters I will highlight how to find and purchase the foreclosures that will lead to outstanding active income stream opportunities.

Besides foreclosures there are many other opportunities to purchase distressed houses. Here are some methods to consider adding to your marketing plan if you want to find dirt cheap houses that may not be listed with realtor's on the MLS (Multiple Listing Service).

1. **Code violators:** When new construction permits began to sharply decline I noticed that many city and county departments began to increase their presence in residential neighborhoods looking for code violators. The zoning and planning inspectors are tasked with being sure they keep work flowing during the slow-down so one easy way is to increase the tagging process of finding code violators. When a home is condemned, it receives a big red tag style sticker on the front door. When driving through neighborhoods, look for homes that have been red-tagged like this one in the photo below.

I know this partially because I have received a couple of letters in the past year about my rental properties. In both cases the letters stated that I had inoperative motor vehicles sitting on my property. When new construction permits were high the inspectors would not have time to mess with mundane issues like this. In both cases I remediated the issues by asking my tenants to resolve the issue and satisfy the housing inspectors so it was not a big deal.

Code violations on a house can be a great resource for finding motivated sellers. If a home is being tagged for being unsafe, open to the public, or a badly leaking roof you can often track down the owners and make them an offer to buy their house. In most cases the owners of the home are not intentionally neglecting their homes, but simply can not afford to keep up the with necessary repairs to keep them in safe operational condition.

One way to find the code violators in your area is to go the city or county offices and request it. Some localities have a list they will gladly share since it is public records. Others may push back and say it is not available; if that is the case you should cite the freedom of information act and ask for the form to formally request it. Once you have the list, drive by the homes and select which ones you have interest in pursuing to purchase and contact the owner via a phone call or letter. You can generally find the owners information on line in the tax assessor's records.

2. **Motivated Landlords** Another great source for finding distressed houses is looking for motivated landlords. Motivated landlords are burned out by their tenants.

You can find burned out landlords in a variety of methods. One way I like to find them is by hanging around the courthouse on the day of evictions. Find a landlord who has just had a hard time with a judge and you will have a motivated seller. Another method I like to use is looking for mattresses on the streets. You know what that means don't you? You are right, it is an indicator of an eviction in process. You can also look for the sherriff's car on the scene. If you find furniture and everything being hauled out of a house and a sheriff on-site you can be sure it is an active eviction and you will find a motivated seller. Simply be a bit bold and tell the owner you might have an interest in buying his house and solving his problem.

You may find out that he owns more than just the one house that he is having a problem with and that could lead to the opportunity of purchasing several of his properties. Always ask if the seller has more houses they would want to sell and you may be lucky to get a package of several houses bundled together at a great price. Below is a picture taken during an eviction where the police and animal control were called in to assist with the tenants loose pit-bull. When you see a situation like this you can bet you have found a landlord ready to sell a house.

Another effective method of finding motivated land-lord sellers is to simply call houses that are for rent. In most cases houses that are "For Rent" are vacant which essentially a non-performing asset for the owner. This method works especially well if the house needs obvious repairs which are leading to the inability of the owner to find a solid tenant.

3. **Short Sales** – As today's toxic loans continue to gob-ble up homeowners, we are seeing a high volume of short sale opportunities. Short sales are homes being sold for less than what is owed on the mortgage bal-ance. As an example if a home owner owes $125,000

on a house, a short sale opportunity may make it possible to purchase the home for $90,000.

There are many factors that influence a lending institutions decision on what they are willing to accept for any given house. Some of the factors include balances owed on the 1st and 2nd mortgage along with owners hardships, etc.

Short sales can be great opportunities in today's marketplace, but also require incredible patience and tremendous amount of work to get approved. I have been working on one for the past four months and still have no counter offer from the lending institution. It is not uncommon to have them take several months to get an approval and be ready to close. In addition to the long wait time, the mounds of documentation required for the short sale process can be intimidating for many people. In general I do not recommend you process your own short sale packages for approval because they consume a tremendous amount of time and often may not work out as you plan. I do recommend you find a good realtor to work with you and it is imperative that your chosen realtor have experience working on short sales and can demonstrate the ability to get offers accepted. Otherwise, you are likely wasting your time working on short sales while missing so many other outstanding opportunities to create income streams today. Short sales are being pushed to help suppress the shadow foreclosure inventory. They can be a source of great opportunities, just understand it can be a long drawn out process.

There are many more ways to easily find motivated sellers and distressed houses to buy at great discounts, but buying foreclosures is the generally the easiest and the best use of your time and resources.

My favorite environment for buying houses is meeting directly with the homeowner at the kitchen table and directly negotiating the sale. It is fast, efficient, and all parties get what they want. When working directly with a seller, I like to make three different offers. At least one of the offers will include seller financing. By making three offers I find that the seller can often make one of them work. If I made just one offer the seller's response can only be yes or no.

One of my favorite parts of buying foreclosures is the speed at which I can make a lot of offers in a short amount of time. Nearly every late spring and early summer I pick a month and commit to making an offer a day on foreclosures. If you want to create income from real estate you will have to buy or control houses and remember you make money when you buy! You cannot buy a house without making offers.

I am not a realtor, but do receive several different multiple listing service (MLS) searches to my email everyday and I scour through them in a lot of detail. I am looking for the worst house in the very best neighborhoods and usually eliminate 99% of all the foreclosures that are for sale. I am looking at list price, pictures to see what work may be needed, and the value or tax assessment to find the most under-priced houses on the market. That remaining one percent of the foreclosures I go after aggressively. I narrow my search on-line and then set up to go look at houses every day in order to make an offer every single day.

When I go to the property and look at the house, I typically know within 15 minutes whether it is a good deal or not. If it is only a "good" deal on the house; I won't be interested in purchasing it as I am really looking for the best one percent available and want to buy only great deals that represent that one percent. If I have to think too long about whether or not it is a great deal then I know for sure it is not the right house for me to buy. For me it has become a buying instinct.

My formal education is Rochester Institute of Technology in Electrical Engineering. RIT is an outstanding Engineering college and they trained me hot and heavy on analyzing everything with formula's and being 100% certain of every detail. When I worked as an engineer for many years I was in environments that were super precise in nature. Some of these included clean rooms where sub micron sized particles were counted in parts per million. Other places included aerospace manufacturing of jet engine parts and yes it is critical that everything is precise. I also worked in telecommunications manufacturing environments for several years with processes where circuit boards are fabricated and components are assembled in very precise environments.

For real estate I had to re-program my thinking to allow me to be quickly decisive and to go with my instincts without having all possible variables covered. This is easier than ever in today's marketplace where distressed property is readily available at deeply discounted prices. The good news is that real estate today is very forgiving since houses are available at such high discounts.

All of the income streams presented in the following chapters will require that you become comfortable with making offers and buying distressed properties to maximize your income. Creating real estate income streams is a team sport and you will need to create a team in order to maximize your income streams.

The first person you will need on your team may be a coach. If you are brand new to investing you may need to seek out the help of a coach. This is someone who can help you take action and meet your goals. If you need a coach be sure to invest your time investigating the background of the person you are seeking to help you. Make sure this individual has a proven track record of helping others achieve their goals and has personally bought, sold, and rented a lot of houses. Not every so-called guru type coach or mentor will be the right fit for you.

You will also need a strong realtor to help you through the process. Notice I didn't say just any realtor. I truly believe that not all realtors are made equal. Although I am sure you know a neighbor, friend, or family member who is already a realtor, they may not be the best one for you work with. Selecting the right realtor is important, just like selecting the right coach and everyone else on your team. The right realtor is an experienced realtor who has completed a number of buying and selling transactions. In other words someone who has experience in today's market. The attitude of your realtor is also very important. Find one who has a positive mindset and who will work to help you achieve your goals. Some realtors specialize in listing foreclosures, others specialize in short sale listings, and others spend their time as buyers agents. You will want to do some investigating and asking for referrals when choosing the realtor for your team.

Another critical person on your team will be a good contractor. A good contractor will have a team supporting him that can include all the trades such as plumbing, electrical, roofing, heat and air, carpentry, painting, flooring, and so on. The reason you need a good contractor is that most of the foreclosures and distressed properties available will need some level of work. If you want more information on how to find a great contractor you should consider reading my other book "*Investing Now*."

Besides a strong realtor and a great contractor you will also want to find someone who can help you manage your houses. If you are looking to build rental income, as detailed in chapter 7, you will want to find someone who can diligently find great tenants and manage your houses. The other option is to do it yourself, but you will need to obtain the skills needed to become a great manager. I believe this is a very important person on your team so you will want to either do it yourself or find a very experienced property manager for your assets.

One more person you will need on your team is an attorney who can help you with contracts and the settlement process when buying or selling houses. There are many attorney's available but you should find one who is great at real estate and who will help you meet your goals. I rely heavily upon my settlement company in Richmond, VA. They are a critical member of my team and help make sure closings are smooth and easy for me.

Finally, the two most important people on your team will be YOU and your partner or spouse. You are doing the right thing by investing in yourself by reading this book. If you have a partner or spouse you will want to pass this book to them once you are done reading it so you can both be on the same page moving forward. If you cannot get your partner or spouse onto the team you will have to struggle with finding success long-term. You will need to get their buy-in on the chosen income streams in order to maximize your success going forward. I would not be successful without the full support of my wife Cheryl. She understands these income streams are opportunities and she is a source of great inspiration for me as we continue to achieve our goals using these streams of income. If you partner or spouse is not on-board yet, do not get discourage as it sometimes takes time to break down the barriers of fear that are very common and natural. The best way to get past the fear is to spend time with successful people and continue to get education along the way.

Today's market is jammed full of distressed properties that provide unprecedented buying opportunities to help set up your income streams for many years to come. Buying foreclosures is an easy way to get started as they provide a lot of inventory in good neighborhoods, nice cul-de-sacs and in great school systems. When the market was hot and appreciating fast, most investors had to buy houses in the ghetto, but in today's market you can buy in great locations. I am looking for that best one percent of houses available and that will often times be the worst house in the best neighborhood. Find that house and you will have a winner.

Chapter 3 Summary

1. Toxic loans made with loose credit, no income verification, and no documentation helped the housing market to _____?

2. Do you have a friend, neighbor or family member who is a realtor? Do they have the experience and skill set to join your team?

3. Is your spouse and/or partner on-board? If not, what can you do to help bring them aboard to meet your income goals?

.

Be the Flipper: Flipping for Large Chunks of Cash

Want some more good news? Today's market is fantastic for flipping houses to first time home buyers. The best part of flipping houses is that it is an income stream that you can add that will provide large chunks of cash. What could you do with some large chunks of cash? Pay down debt, start saving for your kids college, boost your retirement, help a family member in need? Yes, everyone could use some large chunks of cash in today's economy and one way to get it is to learn to flip houses.

Now that you know flipping houses can provide nice chunks of cash for your income stream, I have to tell you that there are a lot of things that must go just right in order to capture this income. But don't worry, because I will provide you with the winning formula.

Flipping houses is an income stream created by buying dirt cheap houses, adding value with the right renovations and then re-selling the home a few months later for more than your invested capital. I will take you through each of these three steps to give you the framework to make it happen. This three step process can be repeated as many times as you want to earn large chunks of cash for your income stream.

<u>Step One:</u> Buy a Dirt Cheap House

I mentioned earlier that you make money in real estate when you buy the house. That being said you will need to gain the skill set necessary to help you recognize a great deal, be able to quickly analyze it, and be prepared to be decisive and ready for action. What does a good deal look like? Is it a house in your own neighborhood, maybe a nice house in an up-scale area or an ocean-front condo? It is possible, but unlikely. Are you looking for the absolute cheapest house in your market, in a war-zone where you would not feel safe at night? No, that is not the winning formula either. Here are the factors and what to look for when searching for the very best deal on a house you can fix and flip.

1. **Location:** You know the saying that real estate is "location, location, location" and I will tell you it is very true. There are some exceptions, but if you want to maximize your profit and minimize your risk you need to be very aware of the location of the house you are looking to flip.

   Finding a house with the right location starts with my simple location litmus test. I have two of the most awesome daughters, Melisa and Carisa, and my location litmus test on location starts with the question - if I would be comfortable sending my daughters to that house at night? As a father, I am always nervous about my daughters being out at night. If a house is in a bad area I would definitely not want them to go there in the dark. If you are nervous about children being safe in a given neighborhood then it is very likely that other families and potential buyers will have the same concern and it will make it tough for you to re-sell that house no matter how great of a job you do on the renovations.

2. **Condition:** Once you find a house in a great location that will appeal to a lot of potential buyers, it will be time to begin to evaluate the condition of the house. If you are not a contractor and do not have experience fixing and flipping houses, then you should look for houses that only require cosmetic repairs. In other words, avoid structural issues, houses with a lot of mold, houses that need an extra bath or a full addition. Instead, look for houses that are structurally sound and have problems that can be easily fixed. Look for houses that only need new make-up, such as paint, flooring, and lighting. Houses that need a light cosmetic fix up are the easiest to fix and have the least amount of risk associated with them.

There are a lot of interacting systems and components in every house and it can sometimes be difficult to know the overall condition of a property based on a brief walk-through. If you are not already an experienced house flipper or contractor, I strongly recommend that you have the house inspected prior to purchase so that you avoid surprises once you actually own the house. You can hire a professional home inspector, but keep in mind that you are looking for the major problems only and not every small issue in the house. If you use a home inspector, let them know you intend to fix up and flip the house and that you need to know the major concerns. If you do not want to hire a home inspector, then you may want to bring along a licensed contractor to help you inspect the house. You will want a contractor familiar with all aspects of the property including roof, heat and air, electrical, plumbing, insulation, etc. You can then have your contractor provide you with an estimate to reno- vate the home to your specifications.

3. **Price:** Along with location and condition, price is ex- tremely important. For me, price is a given in the suc- cess equation. Without the right price I will not buy any house regardless of location or condition. There are two different prices that you need to fully understand and they are the price you can buy at and the price you can sell at.

   Your goal is to buy dirt cheap, add value with ren- ovations and then resell the house for a profit which will become your income stream. You need to know the after-repair value before you buy a house to flip. Remember, you make your money when you buy, so it is critical you buy the right house for the right price. The after-repair value is the price you expect to sell the house for when renovations are complete. You will need to rely on your team members to help you to determine that price. The after repair value is deter- mined by pulling comparables of similar houses. It can be tricky to accurately pull these comparables since your house will be gorgeous and beautifully renovat- ed when complete.

   The price you can buy the house for is also very critical. The list price of the house is only an indicator of what the seller will take for the house and it is just a starting point. You need to determine how much you can pay for the house and you can do that with one simple calculation called loan to value. Here is the magic financial recipe you should strive for when purchasing a home to flip:

Loan to value: This is the ratio of your total investment to the After Repair Value of the house

After repair value: ARV – The price you hope to sell the house for once renovations are complete. For this example assume the ARV is $100,000

Renovation costs: This is your budgeted renovation price. For this example assume renovation cost is $20,000

Sales price: This is the price you can buy the house for. For this example assume sales price is $40,000

The renovation cost + Sales Price is your total capital investment in the property

Total investment of $60,000 = Sales price of $40,0000 + Renovation Costs of$20,0000

ARV (After Repair Value) = $100,000

A good rule of thumb is that you do not want to exceed a 60% LTV (Loan to value)

LTV = Total investment /ARV * 100
60% = $60,000 / $100,000

In this example it works out to 60 percent Loan to Value (LTV). At 60 percent you will have a 40 percent gross margin on your sale. Remember though that other expenses will need to come out of that 40 percent such as real estate commission, utilities, etc. If your loan to value exceeds 60 percent you will begin to add risk to income stream. 60 percent is very much achievable in today's real estate market and will provide you with enough gross margin to provide you with a nice profit once the home is sold.

The bottom line on choosing the right house to flip is to do a quick analysis to be sure you do not exceed 60 percent LTV. Keep the analysis simple but be accurate with your projections of After Repair Value and Renovation Costs. Do not stress over the analysis and do not get emotionally attached to the house you are going to flip. If the house you are considering purchasing to flip is below 60 percent Loan to Value, then keep looking for another house that will fit your buying model.

Step Two: Add Value with the right renovations

Now that you have found the perfect house that meets your financial model and is located in the right location you are set to embark on the renovations.

If you are not already an experienced flipper or licensed contractor I hope you took my advice in step one and bought a house that needs only cosmetic type updates. If you choose a house with serious structural issues, excessive mold or in need of additional bathrooms or additions you will have more work to do than those renovation houses needing cosmetic updates so plan on the renovation taking longer and your holding costs being higher for your flip. Here are some quick flip renovations that will add the most value to the house you are purchasing.

Exterior Curb Appeal

The exterior of the house is extremely important. When potential buyers pull up to the curb or pull into the driveway you want the house to have sufficient curb appeal to draw them right in so they can see how gorgeous the inside of the house is.

Getting the house ready on the outside could be as simple as a power wash and landscape update or it could include these steps as well:

1. **Front door** – The front door is the focal point when a buyer pulls up to the house. We have found that nicely painted red doors help sell houses. If the door is old and ugly, you can easily install a nice door with a simple insert for a reasonable price. Be sure the entire entrance area is crisp and clean for your potential buyers.

2. **Driveway** – Be sure that it is clearly defined and maintained. You can easily add a fresh coat of seal coating to freshen it up. If it is a gravel driveway you may need to bring in a new load of gravel.

3. **Front of house** – Be certain to clean all the windows, power wash the house if needed and repaint the trim to freshen it up. If the siding is all banged up or rotting, you may need to install new vinyl siding. If you have a front porch, be sure the porch flooring is solid and the rails looks great.

4. **Roof** – A bad or ugly roof is a red flag to potential buyers. If needed, install the new roof. If you have heavy stains on the roof you can have it lightly power washed with chemicals to freshen it up.

5. **Yard** – The yard is critical and must be clean. All the leaves must be gone, weeds removed, bushes trimmed, new shrubs planted, grass mowed and fresh mulch installed. The yard is a lot of manual work, but one of the best paybacks on your investment. You want the yard and the entire outdoor space to sparkle so that all potential buyers want to jump out of their car and see what you did on the inside.

Inside Appeal

The first step inside the front door is very important so be sure the view of your property from inside the front door is fantastic. The interior needs to be very neutral to appeal to the most buyers possible.

Walls, ceilings and trim

The walls, ceilings and trim need to look brand new. If you buy a house with a wall of mirrors or heavily textured walls or ceilings you need to arrange to get rid of them. If you buy a house with tons of dings and dents, you will need to be sure to fix all your walls. If you buy a house with wallpaper it needs to be stripped and prepped for painting. If you buy a house with old, loose dark brown paneling you will need to get rid of it and float the walls with join compound to prep for paint. Below you will see a photo of Jose who always does an outstanding job helping me make old walls look brand new. You get my point that the appearance of your walls is very important.

It is costly to properly fix and repair drywall or plaster, but it is not an area that you can short-cut. There are some exceptions such as being able to paint paneling if it is in great shape and tight on the walls, but these are exceptions and most often you will need to properly prep the walls so they look brand-new. Once the walls are set be sure you are ready to paint all surfaces with neutral color paint. You can use one color throughout the house or paint different colors in different rooms. Do not cut corners by painting the ceiling, walls and trim the same color. It is important to have the right contrast between the walls, ceiling and the trim. You can make the trim pop right out by using a good quality semi-gloss white.

Flooring

There are a lot of great choices in flooring to consider. My personal favorite is to simply refinish wood floors. Most wood floors can be sanded regardless of how bad they look. The exception is pet stains, but even pet stains can be concealed by choosing the right colored stain. I love all wood floors, but my personal favorite is in really old houses where the original hart pine floors can be refinished. Below is a picture of Brad helping refinish stairs in a historic style house in Richmond, VA.

Besides refinishing wood floors, I sometimes find that an engineered style wood laminate floor can be effective at creating the look and feel of a wood floor at a great price. I also will selectively use carpeting in bedrooms as needed. In the kitchen and baths your main choices are vinyl and ceramic. Ceramic is a fantastic product but costs a lot more than the vinyl alternative. For laundry areas you can some-times save even more money and use a VCT tile.

Kitchen and baths

By far the most the important rooms in your home are the kitchens and baths We all know that women buy the houses so be sure to have great space for your kitchen and baths. Kitchens need to be bright and remodeled. They can be expensive but the investment will definitely pay off. No one wants to buy an old grungy kitchen like the one in this photo.

Sometimes you can save money on your renovations by refreshing your existing cabinets with fresh paint, new counter top, new sink and new cabinet hardware. Many times though you will need to demo the existing kitchen, design a new layout that will include brand new cabinets, counter tops, and a nice back splash. Either way, you will want to be sure to have brand new appliances and you should strongly consider using stainless steel matching appliances. May old kitchens do not have dishwashers so be certain to include it in your new kitchen.

In the bathrooms you will likely need new fixtures including vanity, lights, faucets and towel bar type accessories. Be sure to replace the toilet if needed. Sometimes you will need to replace the entire bathtub or even add a new bathroom to the house. See picture below of Mark working on the plumbing of a new bathtub. Be sure you are comfortable with your team's skills including heat and air, plumbing and electrical. These services are critical and your team members must have sufficient knowledge and experience to get the jobs done right, on-time, and on budget.

The interior of your home needs to be extremely clean when complete. A lot of dust, debris and trash is created during renovation and it will need an industrial strength cleaning when complete. Once the house is complete, be sure to stage it to help the buyer see the whole potential of your house. Staging can include a nice shower curtain, towels, and simple accessories strategically placed to make your house gorgeous. Below is a photo of my daughter, Carisa, helping us clean and stage a home.

Once your home is completely renovated you will be ready to develop your sales strategy to sell your home so you can collect your profit.

Step 3: Sell the house for profit

To effectively sell your home you will need to enlist the help of a skilled realtor. It seems that everyone knows a realtor or has a neighbor or a friend who is a realtor. The fact is though, that just knowing a realtor does not mean that person is the right pick for helping you sell your house. When looking for a realtor, be sure to find one who is skilled at marketing beyond the power of the multiple listing service (MLS). Marketing today is much different than it was just a few years ago. In the past realtors relied heavily on advertising in newspapers, but today it can be highly effective to harness the power of the Internet and social media to connect buyers and sellers together. Be sure that the realtor you bring to your team is highly skilled in marketing and will work hard to connect your house with a buyer so you can you collect your profit that will set up your income stream.

In addition to getting a great realtor, there is a lot of marketing that you can do personally to help sell your home. These include creating flyers, posting the house for sale on Craigslist, and using social media to broadcast that the house is for sale. Be sure to take a video of your home and place it into a YouTube channel. When you place your Craigslist ads you can provide a link directly to your video. Potential buyers love watching videos of homes they are considering taking a closer look at. One time I met a couple to show them a house. I offered to show them through the house and she told me it was not necessary as she has watched my YouTube video many times and already knows her way around the house. You see my point that YouTube video marketing is critical to your overall marketing strategy when selling a house.

One other incentive that I always recommend is that you pay some closing cost assistance for the buyer and provide the selling realtor with a bonus on top of their three percent commission. I want to reward the buyer and selling realtor to help my houses stand out from the others that are available on the market.

Flipping houses can create a nice income stream that provides you with large chunks of cash. It is important to know that many things must be done just right in order to flip houses today. The process starts with buying the right house, then you need to hire a great contractor and manage the renovations, finally you will need to add a fantastic realtor to your team who can effectively market your home to qualified buyers.

Here is a typical time line:

Flip Time Line to Cash

30 – 45 days Purchase and renovate a home
45 - 85 days Market and sell your home
85 - 120 days Closing process with the new buyer
and collect check

If you buy the right house, do the right renovations, and have a solid marketing plan to get it sold you should be able to complete the cycle in about four months.

Flipping houses became very popular when the housing market boomed and network television began airing reality tv shows on the subject. The fact is that today, the market for flipping is excellent. This is in large part because first time homebuyers are still buying a lot of houses with very low interest rates and plenty of government grants. What makes today's market even better for flipping is that the price you can buy a house for has dropped significantly which makes it easier to purchase distressed houses.

If you would like to learn more about this income stream, please consider purchasing my book *Investing Now* This book is completely dedicated to the process of flipping houses. You can find additional resources available on my main web site at www.investingnownetwork.com. Please stop by, stay a while, and be sure to sign up for my newsletter.

Chapter 4 Summary

1. What are the three steps of flipping a house?

   1. _____

   2. _____

   3. _____

2. What is LTV and why is it important?

3. What color front door helps to sell a house?

4. What is the typical time-frame from start to end?

5. Where can you get more information on flipping houses?

Chapter 5

BE THE WHOLESALER: SELL HOUSES TO INVESTORS

You may be wondering, "How can I wholesale a house?" The reason you are wondering is because it is a well kept secret among real estate investors and never written about in mainstream books. The fact is that it is a great way to get into real estate investing with no money and your credit score does not matter. There is serious potential to create significant income if you apply these concepts to wholesale houses.

Wholesaling houses is a lot like flipping houses, but without having to do any renovation work and without having to own the house. There are fewer moving pieces in the transaction than when you flip houses. There is also a smaller investment risk when wholesaling houses. Less work, less moving pieces, and less risk is what makes wholesaling houses a very nice income stream.

How would you like to sell a house you don't yet formally own and buy it with money you don't yet have? That is why wholesaling real estate works great as an income stream. It is wholesaling houses that allowed me to escape corporate America in 2006. I wholesaled over 100 houses in 2007 which provided a very nice, consistent income stream that allowed me to leave my job. I learned to buy houses directly from the owner's without needing a realtor. I then compiled an extensive list of investors to sell my houses to. I would conduct investor bus tours, load about 55 investors onto a bus and go sell six to eight houses on a Saturday. I would make the investor bus tours a fun and educational event. My wife Cheryl, daughter's Melisa and Carisa and my brother David all helped me with the investor bus tour event. We typically sold six to eight houses in one day during the bus tours and had a goal that everyone has fun.

High volume wholesaling is a lot of work and you may not want to wholesale 100 houses per year, but if you are looking for an alternate real estate income stream you should strongly consider wholesaling in either low or high volume.

Essentially the way wholesaling works is that you first find a distressed property owned by a motivated seller. A motivated seller is someone who has to sell in the near future. You then obtain an option to buy the seller's house with the understanding that you will only purchase the house once you find another investor that you can sell the house to. Once you identify an investor willing to buy the house, you can assign your contract or sell your option for a fee. Here are the steps to the entire process.

Wholesaling houses process

Step 1- Control a dirt cheap house from a motivated seller

Earlier in the book I gave some specific methodologies for finding your own dirt cheap houses directly from sellers.

The key to wholesaling is to find really cheap houses. I learned a lot about wholesaling from Jackie Lange and she drilled it into my head to go slumming to find the absolute cheapest houses. Once I took her advice, I began to find lots of really cheap houses. These were typically houses that realtors would not want to deal with. The cheapest houses have the least amount of commission, are typically badly neglected and hard to sell as-is.

If you are a realtor I know you would rather sell a $300,000 house rather than a $30,000 house because your earnings are way higher for the same amount of work. The other reason realtors do not like dirt cheap houses is that they come with a lot of headaches in the shape of deferred maintenance and repairs. They also might be full of junk and generally not looking so great from the curb. This is part of the reason wholesaling is such a nice niche income stream because realtors would much rather work on higher end homes rather than lower-end homes that need work.

Once you have identified a house that is in distress and has a motivated seller you will need to negotiate a sales price and use an option to lock it up contractually. I like to start the price discussion by asking the owner how much they want for the house. I do not like to lead off the conversation by throwing out a price because their price could be lower than I expect. I always try to get them to commit first in the discussion and have found this works great. Once they commit to an initial price, I remind them that not using a realtor will save them six percent commission. I then highlight some of the problems with the house such as the bad roof, sloping floors, old kitchen, and that kind of thing. I don't want to put the house down explicitly but I do want them to know that I understand the conditions presented and that there will be a lot of expenses associated with the repairs. Normally these types of houses are not financeable by banks in today's credit market so I point that out to them and ask if they can help improve their asking price knowing they do not pay realtor commission and that I will buy the house as-is in a cash sale. Most often they will dramatically reduce their price before I reveal the price I am willing to pay for the house.

Step 2 – Sign a contract

Once you have negotiated a price you need to sign a contract to reflect the agreed upon price and terms of the deal. When wholesaling I always recommend using an option contract because it greatly reduces the risk of the transaction. Real estate options sound a lot more complicated than they really are so I want to clarify what an option is and how to effectively use one when wholesaling real estate.

An option is simply a right to buy a property at a given price. That is not complicated is it? The part that confuses most people is "the right to buy." In exchange for the seller to grant you the right to buy their house, you will exchange some consideration in the form of cash at the time of signing the contract. The exchange of the consideration is similar to an earnest money deposit on a regular real estate transaction. The consideration does not need to a lot of money, I would suggest you make it between $25 - $100.

Once the option contract is signed, the wholesaler has contractual option rights and equitable interest in the property and that allows the wholesaler to take two courses of action:

1. If the wholesaler successfully finds an investor buyer willing to pay a higher price than the option contract, then he can sell or assign his option to the new buyer. This is one way a wholesaler creates an income stream on a house he does not yet own.

2. If the wholesaler cannot find an investor to buy the property he has two choices. First, he can try to renegotiate his price or let the seller know that he will not exercise his option. Remember, the wholesaler only has the *option* to buy, which is not a legal obligation to buy the house. The only one who has a legal obligation is the seller, should you exercise your option to buy he legally has to sell you the house. This is why an option contract works great for wholesaling houses.

A more risky form of wholesaling involves not using a formal option contract. Instead the buyer uses a regular real estate purchase contract but uses an easy contingency such as subject to "buyers partner's approval," "acceptable home inspection," or some variation thereof.

I strongly suggest that you be completely honest with the seller of the home and tell them your intentions to resell the house to an investor in your network and that if you cannot find an investor who wants their home then you will not be able to buy their home. I know many people teaching on wholesaling do not train on the honest principals, but in the end our reputation is not replaceable if a deal does not work out. I always believe in having no surprises and that way no one has false expectations.

Given the high volume of foreclosure inventory I want to highlight how you can wholesale a foreclosure, but under stand your risk is a little higher when working to wholesale a foreclosure. Simply, find an incredibly cheap foreclosure; make a low offer, with an inspection contingency and a 45 – 60 day close time. If the offer gets accepted you will have a short window in which you will be able to market to find a new buyer for the house.

Step 3 – Find an investor to buy your interest in the house

Now you have found a cheap house, negotiated the price and terms and signed an option contract with the seller that gives you equitable interest and control of the property. It is time to generate income based on your interest in the house. You generate the income in one of three ways:

1. Sell your option to another investor for a fee.

2. Assign your contract to another investor. If you assign your contract, the new buyer essentially takes control of the property and will buy it with no further involvement from you.

3. Sell the house to an investor and do a double or simultaneous closing. If you elect to take this path you remain in the transaction right through closing and will be in the chain of title forever. As an example if you have an contract to buy a house for $40,000 and you find an investor willing to buy the house for $55,000 you can make $15,0000 gross profit on that one transaction. The better the deal you make with the seller, then the more profit potential you have when selling to another investor which is why learning to negotiate is a critical part of wholesaling.

I wholesaled a lot of houses by building a very large buyer network. If you find great deals, learn to control them contractually, you can then begin to market the house to other potential buyers. Here are some ways to begin to find investor buyers for your properties and begin to build your own buyers list of investors to whole-sale your houses.

1. Real Estate Investors Associations and clubs.

Most clubs meet at least once per month and I know some that meet every week, like the one in Roanoke, VA. These meetings have investors attending that would like to buy great deals so package your deal together and go to the meeting prepared to find your new buyer for your house. If someone appears interested, be sure to collect their name, phone, and email so you can contact them in the future.

2. Bandit Signs

I mentioned earlier how effective bandit signs are when looking to buy houses and the same is true when looking to sell houses. It does not need to be a fancy sign, in fact you can get blank yellow signs and holders at your local hardware store. Use a big marker and just write something like this on your sign to attract buyers:

Half Price House
For Sale
Call or Text XXX-XXX-XXXX

Plan to put these signs in strategic locations near the house you are looking to sell and you will find that potential buyers will contact you. When they do contact you, be ready to collect their contact information including email and phone number. Also ask them for the type and location of houses they are looking for and how they plan to pay for them.

One big change I have noted on buying and selling houses over the past year or so is that some people would prefer to contact me via SMS text messaging than calling me on the phone. The world of mobile marketing is rapidly changing and you need to be ready to change with it. One easy way to be prepared is to allow potential buyers and sellers to text you rather than calling.

3. Reverse bandit sign marketing

Now that you know the secrets of using bandit signs to find buyers, you will not be surprised you can use the reverse methods to find even more buyers. In addition to placing bandit signs to find buyers you can easily find even more buyers by calling other people's signs. Chances are that some of the people placing signs are not just wholesaling houses and they are just marketing to find their own houses and could use your help to find a house to buy.

4. Internet Marketing

The Internet is a world class resource for generating leads including finding wholesale buyers for your houses. Craigslist, eBay, and social media connections are all great ways to get your message out that you have a dirt cheap house with a lot of equity to sell.

When posting on the Internet it is ideal if you can give several different ways for potential buyers to contact you. These should include email, phone, text, and a link to your website .

Here are some key words to use when posting for buyers on the Internet: dirt cheap, super cheap, tons of equity, investor special, handyman special, half price.

Also be sure to include pictures of your houses when posting as that will help increase the leads that you will receive.

Try working these key words into your title and into the content of your postings and you will find that buyers will start to call you looking for a house to buy.

5. Lenders

Hard money lenders have money and funds lined up for real estate investors, but often times their borrowers cannot find their own houses to buy. Find out who the hard money lenders in your area are, begin to build a relationship with them and you will begin to find out who is buying houses in your local market. The nice thing about these leads is that they are already warm in that they have their funding established and just need a house to buy in order to move forward.

Each person who contacts you is a potential buyer either right now or in the future. Be sure to get their contact information including name, email, and phone number and ask if you can add them to your exclusive buyers list. If they are not interested in this particular house you have for sale, be sure to find out what type, price, and location of a house they want. Once you know exactly what they want, you can treat that as an order and go find a great property for them to buy from you.

You will find that wholesaling in volume becomes like most other order fulfillment type businesses in that you will have buyers and orders to fulfill. For me, the very first wholesale transaction was the hardest. I could find houses, but then not find a buyer. I could find a buyer and then not find a house. I didn't give up though and eventually I got the whole cycle synchronized so that I had a lot of houses and a lot of buyers and just put the two together to create a lot of deals.

Step 4 – Collect your cash

Wholesaling can be an excellent income stream without having to do the work involved with a house rehab, without credit and without needing any cash. Wholesaling allows you to operate in the middle of a deal and collect a fee for putting the ultimate buyer and seller together. Typical wholesale fee's will range from $2,000 - $7,000 per transaction. You will be able to make even more when you have a really great deal on your option to buy and a strong cash buyer. There are a few different ways you can get paid wholesaling:

Assignment

A real estate option can be sold for a fee or assigned to another investor for a fee. That fee is your pay for putting the deal together. You can assign your contract or sell your option with a simple one-page contract that specifies the terms.

Sell the house

You can also just resell the house, even before you formally own it. Once you have an option or a contract to buy a house you have equitable interest in the property. Be sure that the current owner will allow you to show the property to prospective buyers and begin marketing to sell the house. Once you have found a new buyer for the property just ratify a new contract between yourself and your new buyer. You can then do either a simultaneous closing or a regular double closing where you buy and sell the house at essentially the same time. The difference between your buy and your sell price is your gross profit on your transaction.

Bird Dogging

One other way to begin creating income quickly is a variation of wholesaling called bird-dogging. A bird dog is the type of dog that accurately leads the hunter to the bird when hunting and the same concept is true with a real estate bird dog.

I have trained and used a lot of bird dogs to help me find houses to buy. I pay my bird dogs between $500 and $1,000 per house they help me find that I can buy. I pay them at closing when I buy or wholesale the house.

In this economy just about everybody knows someone who is in trouble on their house. The nice thing about bird dogging is that it allows you to create income without needing to find the end-buyer in the transaction. If you want to start off as a bird dog you can find a wholesaler to work with you pretty easily. If you can supply great proper-ties to buy you will find yourself with a nice income stream while learning the business.

When I was wholesaling in high volume I relied on my bird dogs to help me find houses for my buyers. I started off training a number of friends and family members to begin searching for houses for me to buy. I showed them how to search for the houses and contact the owners. Once the owner expressed interest in selling their house I would meet them and make an offer. My brother David became especially good at finding distressed houses and tracking down owners for me. David became a novice skip-tracer in that he was good at using the Internet to find phone numbers of potential buyers. Once he had their number, he would simply call the owner and tell them he is looking to buy a house in a given area and ask the owner if they know anyone looking to sell. David helped me buy a lot of houses and received a lot of bird dog fees for helping me find houses to buy.

Bird-dogging can be an excellent introductory income stream for a new investor or someone looking to get started in real estate part-time. There is zero risk involved and once you become good at finding motivated sellers a lot of new real estate investing doors will open for you and lead to additional income streams.

Wholesaling is a great way to get started in creat-ing income in real estate with minimal experience. Three reasonably easy steps and you have a profit of $2,000 - $7,000. If you want to take an even easier road toward wholesaling, consider starting as a bird-dog and charge a $500 - $1,000 fee for every house great deal that you find. As you get more comfortable you will be able to put multiple deals together and create a nice income stream without cash or credit. Wholesaling is how I started, but you need to learn to be comfortable as a wheeler-dealer and generate your cash flow in the middle of as many deals as you can.

CHAPTER 5 SUMMARY

1. Wholesaling is a lot like flipping houses, but _____ having to do the renovation work.

2. Step one in wholesaling houses is to find a dirt cheap house for sale by a _____ seller.

3. Step two in wholesaling houses is to sign a _____.

4. Step three in wholesaling houses is to find a _____.

5. What are the five ways to find investor buyers who you can wholesale to?

   _____

   _____

   _____

   _____

   _____

BE THE LANDLORD: RENTAL INCOME STREAMS

Liabilities, assets, and cash flow

Sometimes it is hard to know how to spend your money. Should you buy a liability such as a car, boat, or maybe a recreational vehicle? What if you take some of your money and buy an income-producing asset? It can be so much fun to go out and get a new car or a new "toy" to give you the fun that you deserve. But, what if you could invest your time, energy. and resources into assets that could provide you with income streams to help you meet your financial goals?

The following illustration was sent to me from a reader of my previous book and it tells the perfect story about the difference between assets, liabilities. and cash flow. I appreciate Bruce Brown sharing this illustration and the picture provided below. It is an excellent illustration of this income stream.

"Buying a house can be cheaper than buying a new car. The price of the house in this picture, including the renovation expense was $300 less than the price

of my 2012 Mitsubishi Gallant. The cash flow that my rental property produces will make my car payment on my Mitsubishi. Four years from now my car is paid off and the cash flow from the house continues... Cha ching!!"... Bruce Brown

Bruce has figured out how to invest in today's real estate market. Purchase income-producing assets without using your own money, without needing a bank, and begin to enjoy the many benefits of positive cash flow. Cars, boats, recreational vehicles, and other liabilities will be depreciating and creating negative cash flow for you, however, if you can focus your energy on positive cash flow and building assets you can strike it rich in today's real estate market.

How many houses would you need to purchase to set you financially free? How much positive rental income would be required so you could quit your job? We are experiencing the greatest transfer of real estate wealth of our generation. Now is the perfect time to establish a real plan to allow you to experience the financial freedom you deserve buying and holding real estate. My advice is to buy houses for the positive cash flow, not to merely build your Real Estate Empire and net-worth. If you focus intensely on cash flow your investments will pay you an income stream every single month and someday if you decide to sell them you will have a potentially big payday at the end when you finally cash-out. The cash flow is the critical piece to your long-term wealth-building plan with real estate. Without positive cash flow you won't be able to hang onto your assets long enough to enjoy that future payday.

How would you like to buy houses and have tenants that you barely know pay for your houses each month? Buying and holding rental property can create long-term wealth, cash flow for today, and huge tax savings in the form of depreciation. So what could possibly be so hard about buying and holding real estate? Oh yes, those tenants! The fear is typically the tenants. Fear that they will not pay their rent, fear that they will trash your house, and fear that you cannot keep up with necessary repairs and improvements. If we overcome those objections are you ready to venture out to buy some rental properties and create an income stream? I hope so, because you will certainly be glad that you did.

I mentioned earlier in the book that my wife Cheryl and I bought our first investment property just a few years after we were married in 1987. My dad worked full-time at an architectural firm and he was also a part-time landlord. He made it look easy so Cheryl and I decided to jump into investing and purchased a duplex on Grant Street in Jamestown, NY.

We bought our duplex for a whopping $21,000. We carefully calculated the expected cash flow based on the rents that we would expect to receive in the 3 bedroom lower apartment and 1 bedroom upper apartment and quickly determined that this must be a great investment for us. From memory we planned for about $800 in monthly rental income against our monthly mortgage of $225. On paper everything looked good, but what happened after we purchased this duplex?

The first thing we learned was that the house needed tons of repairs and we did not have the capital available to handle all the repairs. I specifically remember that the space heater in the upstairs apartment did not work. In some climates maybe you could get by without good heat, but not Jamestown, NY. In January, the average low is 15 degrees. I remember many days where it was well below zero in January and to make it worse; Jamestown is in direct line for lake effect snow from Lake Erie and on average receives 100 inches of snow each year. You can imagine our shock when we found out there was no working heat in the upstairs apartment. Shortly after that was resolved with a new space heater, we found out that the boiler in the basement for the lower apartment was also not working very well. We didn't have money to fix that one so I purchased books on boilers and taught myself how to fix it and keep it going with minimal expense. The repairs continued in many forms and we had a hard time keeping up with the expenses associated with owning our $21,000 duplex that cash flowed like crazy on my piece of notebook paper. We learned that buying the absolute cheapest house in a questionable area of town might not have been the great investment that it appeared.

The next lesson we learned very quickly was that we were lousy landlords. In fact, I knew nothing about a rental application, tenant screening or how to manage property. My lack of knowledge led me directly to the school of hard knocks for landlords. My idea of finding tenants was to place an ad in the local paper and rent the apartment to the first person who had some cash for me. I found a generic fill in the blank style lease agreement and got the tenant to sign it even though I didn't even know what it meant.

Things went fine until the tenants didn't pay us their rent. I certainly had no idea how the eviction process worked or what I could or could not do to get my rent. Not knowing the laws led me to breaking a few rules while working to collect my rent. I learned quickly how to out-smart those tenants and get my rent or get them out of my apartments.

Managing this duplex was so frustrating that my wife made me promise we would never try it again and refused to ever consider becoming a landlord again. We moved to Virginia in 1998 and absolutely had to sell this duplex prior to our move. It was then that we learned to sell it on a land contract with the new buyer having a refinance lined up simultaneous with that closing which netted us some money and more importantly freed our souls from our first investment property.

So why would I share that story in a book about encouraging people to buy and hold rental properties? I want to emphasize three points:

It is OK to fail

We made some of the same mistakes that many other investors make when first starting out. The first mistake was just buying the cheapest duplex we could find. Buying the cheapest duplex led us into a pit of constant repairs. We were also significantly under capitalized in this venture. The house was cheap for multiple reasons including the overall condition and the location. There is no real ghetto or war zone in Jamestown, NY but this was far from a prime neighborhood that would attract the very best tenants. Having a not-so-great property in a not-so-great location led us to attract not-so-great tenants. See the connections in this story? Did we fail on our very first investment property? I would say that we did, but in the process we learned some very valuable lessons via the school of hard knocks.

Learn before you earn

I mentioned before that I am now a lifetime learner. I earned my Masters Degree in Engineering Management, but more importantly I have never stopped learning. I am interested in many different things so it is easy for me to never stop learning. The real mistake I made as a very young investor was not buying the property, but rather that I should have learned before I tried to earn. If I had properly learned about buying the right house, landlording, and investing I could have avoided the many headaches that I created for myself. In fact it was some of my experiences with this house that led me to become a lifetime learner in the first place. I resolved to never being unprepared like that again.

It all turns out good in the end

Yes, our story turned out fine in the end. My wife did swear we would never become landlords again and she kept that mantra for a number of years. She came back around after we had learned the process of being a successful landlord. I have to thank Dave Tilney and a few others for teaching me to systematize my property management process. There is a big difference between being a regular landlord and being a successful landlord. I had to invest in myself and learn how to buy and manage property in order turn my investing career around. Once I learned how to buy the right houses, in the right locations, and attract the right tenants our landlording life became much easier. We then took the time to systematize the entire process and now it runs very smoothly.

Buying and holding rental property can lead you to long term wealth and nice monthly income streams when done correctly. That is the reason I shared my own story so you could see the mistakes I made. I will now share some of the secrets to landlording that make the whole process much easier and actually an enjoyable income stream for you.

Buy the right property for your income stream

There are many different investment asset classes you can choose from for your rental income streams. Here are some of them you may want to consider:

1. Single family homes
2. Multi-family property
3. Commercial
4. Land

You know that we bought the cheapest duplex available and it didn't work out too well for us. Some experienced investors create fantastic income streams buying rental properties in the war-zones and renting to section 8 government subsidized tenants. My point is that it did not work out well for us and our inexperience compounded the challenges that we experienced. If you are new to investing, please consider this a warning and if you choose to invest in the war-zones you will need to be fully prepared for that investing model.

1. **Single family homes** – This is my favorite asset class for real estate investing. It is the class I have done the best at, with the least amount of work and least amount of risk. I love single family homes because they are very easy to rent to good tenants. Many tenants start-off renting apartments and eventually want more space, privacy and a yard, that is when they start to look for a house to rent.

    I have found that tenants renting my houses stay longer and are easier for me to manage. I also find I have less emergency calls and repairs to the property. I also like the single families because I find they are easier to sell when needed. As Walter Wofford says, "some houses are trading sardines and some are real keepers." You will quickly learn which of your houses will be with you for many, many years and which ones can be traded out of your inventory. One of the nice features of single family homes is that you can sell or trade the ones that do not meet your long-term goals.

2. **Multi-family property** – Multi-family property is any housing which contains more than one unit so that

includes duplex's, triplex, quads all the way up to hundreds of units. I have friends who absolutely love multi-family investment properties. One reason they love it so much is that every front door they own is a potential tenant who will pay them rent every month. Because there are so many doors, apartments, and tenants the overall cash flow can be fantastic when the property is fully rented to great tenants who pay every month. One of the challenges with multi-family is keeping it fully occupied with rent paying tenants.

Having so many tenants can also lead to plenty of drama. For me, I had a lot of great tenants and one really offensive tenant who created drama for all the rest of them in my quad. This tenant was challenged in many ways and she made everyone around pay the costs of her challenges. For example, in the middle of the night she would start dropping a bowling ball onto her floor. Can you imagine how that sounded to the tenants renting below her? She also had many other odd tricks like hiding in the bushes spying on other tenants and so on. You can imagine the drama this created in our multi-family property and it resulted in quite a few visits from the local police. My father-in-law also helps me with property management and I can tell you that he lost a lot of hair from this tenant and the remaining hair he did have turned grayer with every challenge from this particular tenant.

She was the single biggest problem tenant that I have ever had to deal with, so what did I do to solve the issue? This tenant in our multi-family investment property was beginning to cause me to become a motivated seller so I packaged the property, rent rolls, calculated the cap rate, and sold it! Multi-family housing can be fantastic cash flow, but it is not for every investor. I suggest that if you want to go into multi-family, plan on paying for a really great property manager so that you can avoid the drama that sometimes comes with it.

3. **Commercial** – Distressed commercial properties are becoming available more frequently than in past years. For that reason, they can work well for the investor who wants to go that direction with their investing models. I have recently seen foreclosed car washes and other buildings that have looked pretty good on paper. If you are looking for some great cash flow you should also consider a mobile home park. Mobile home parks have several different income streams available to the owners and can be fantastic investments. In general, I believe that commercial opportunities can be a higher risk and higher reward model. The risk comes from our poor economy and the struggle to find quality business tenants. The upside reward comes from the prices that have dramatically dropped in the recent years. One other form of commercial I personally like is mixed-use which combines commercial and multi-family investments. For me, this can be the best of both worlds for investors looking for strong cash flow without having to rely entirely on finding business tenants.

Finding the best tenants for your income stream

Now that you know which asset class you want to invest in you need to understand what your potential tenants are looking for so that you attract the best of the best. Two items that are very important to finding great tenants are location and condition of the housing you are providing.

Location – Location can be a delicate balancing act for investors buying rental properties. The reason for that is because typically the cheaper properties with the least amount of capital investment will often lead to the greatest overall return on investment. Look at the investment and return on investment of these two houses:

House one: Purchased for $50k, rents for $875 per month

House two: Purchased for $100k, rents for $950 per month

Assuming both houses are 3 bedrooms with 2 bathrooms and in the same overall condition, the main contributor to house one being $50k less than house two is likely to be the location. House one has a much better rate of return than house two and in fact you could buy two of the first houses and create income of $1,725 for the same investment as house two. In summary, you need to balance your investments with the best combination of price, location, and house available in your marketplace in order to maximize your return on investment.

If you can purchase a house in a nice area with decent schools and then renovate to make it look nice, you will attract the best tenants for your investment. I like to buy houses to rent in suburb type, working class neighborhoods with decent school systems. This is the formula that works best for me to attract the kind of tenants I want to work with. I also advocate spending the necessary time and money up-front to renovate the house to attract good quality tenants. Be sure it shows nicely and is very clean. When I market the house to find my new tenant, I am hoping that multiple tenants will want to rent my house so that I can adequately qualify and choose the one that I want to work with.

How to find great tenants

Once the house looks nice, it is time to find the best possible tenants for your investment. I like to use my corporate background when finding tenants. I have had hundreds of people working for me which brought plenty of experience hiring new employees. I approach finding tenants the same way I would recruit for good employees in corporate America. When I would hire new employees I would have a job description, which included the job responsibilities. The same is true when I am looking for new tenants. My tenant job description includes the following:

1. Pay rent on-time, every month
2. Take care of the house (asset)

If you could find tenants who would will pay you on-time and take good care of your houses would you still be afraid to rent houses? Of course not, so the house location and condition are important and so is your ability to find the right tenant to work with. My mindset as a landlord is the same as when I had a lot of people working for me. I have a job open and advertise to fill the job. People send in a resume or complete an application; we would screen the applications, perform background checks, and eventually choose the best candidate for our job. Once the new employee is hired, I expect him/her to come to work on time every day and complete the tasks and responsibilities we have given him.

For me, it is the same process when you become a landlord. I market to find tenants, have them complete a rental application, screen the application, check credit and criminal back ground, and select the best tenant available. My goal for the new tenant is to find the one who can best fill my job description which includes paying rent on-time every month and taking care of my assets (the house they are renting).

Marketing to find tenants

There are generally three types of tenants you can choose from. The tenants who meet the job description you establish, the dead beats, and the government subsidized tenants.

1. Deadbeats

Deadbeats can sometimes appear as great tenants so you do need to be careful. A deadbeat tenant is one who will cause you problems either paying rent and/or will trash your house. That is the bad news, but the good news is that there are more great tenants available right now than in the previous several years. Yes, the rental market has gotten a lot stronger so it is easier to find better tenants right now. The way to avoid deadbeat tenants is to carefully screen their rental application, call all previous landlords, verify their employment, get copies of their paystubs, pull credit, and check criminal background. If you are diligent in your screening and verifying all information you can avoid the deadbeat tenants.

2. **Government subsidized tenants**

Also known as the section 8 program, this government program dates back to the Housing Act of 1937. Section 8 pays rent for over three million low income households. There are a variety of section 8 programs available to low income tenants but the most popular is the voucher choice program. This program will pay either a portion of the tenants rent or all of the tenants rent depending on the individual tenants financial situation.Most tenants pay about thirty percent of their take home adjusted income for section 8 housing. The adjusted income takes into account deductions for dependents, disabilities, and other medical expenses. If the tenant is unemployed or has a several children they may become eligible to have their entire rent paid by this program.

Most landlords either love or hate the section 8 program. They love it because they do not need to worry about getting their rent paid. They also love receiving their rent on time every single month. They also love it because they can charge a lot for their rent.

One of the reasons that some Landlords do not like Section 8 is the government regulation. They really do not want the government involved with their rental properties. The government places regulation on all property in their section 8 program. The regulation includes a safety inspection when the tenant moves in and then on-going inspections at least annually. Following the inspection process you will need to fix every item on their list before the tenant is approved for move-in.

Another primary concern is with the quality of the tenant. They fear that the section 8 tenants will be rough on their property, not properly maintain the house, etc. One way to minimize this issue is to fully screen the section 8 tenant prospects the same way that you do for non-section 8 tenants. You need to pull criminal background checks, call previous landlords, and check everything regardless if the tenant is in the section 8 program or not.

3. **Great tenants**

Some people do not believe that there are great tenants, but I am here to share some good news with you. Yes, there are great tenants. These are the tenants that fulfill your job description, pay rent on time every month, take good care of your house, stay for many years, and leave you alone. The question is what are the methods for finding these tenants. The key to finding great tenants starts with having good housing in desirable locations so that the very best tenants will want to live in your house. Beyond having a good property, here are some keys to marketing for tenants.

Craigslist - Craigslist was started in 1995 by Craig Newman. It began as an email distribution list, thus the name Craigslist, among friends highlighting events in San Francisco. The first category Craig added was during the apartment shortage in the mid-1990s. The first city beyond San Francisco was added in 2000 when Boston was the first of nine new cities added that year.

Craigslist then began a web-based service in 1996 and has now grown to over 700 cities in more than 70 countries worldwide. Craigslist was the first site on the Internet that began to connect people in need with people who have something to offer. Relationships between those in need and those who have something to give began to develop. The service was expanded to include forums and a classified ad style marketplace. The site now serves more than 20 billion page views per month which makes it one of the most widely used websites in the world.

One of the first needs that Craigslist fulfilled was housing – specifically connecting tenants with available apartments. Today, the "apts / housing for rent" section of Craigslist is extremely active with postings and the "housing wanted" section also gets quite a few posts every day. The opportunity for finding great tenants by marketing on Craigslist is excellent.

When posting your houses and apartments for rent, be sure to use a catchy title and a good description of the features of your housing. Craigslist allows users to post up to four photos of their housing. Be sure to use quality pictures, which show the front, kitchen, bath and living spaces. With a great title, solid description and pictures be sure to include your contact information so potential tenants can contact you. To make it easy for potential tenants, you can give them three ways to contact you:

1. Email
2. Phone
3. Text

I highly recommend you get a Google voice phone number to use when searching for and working with tenants. They are free, can forward to your phone, provide you with visual voice mail, and keep your primary phone number private from everyone who contacts you. If you have a website dedicated to your rental properties, be sure to link to it direct from the Craigslist postings.

Besides Craigslist, there are other quality sites for connecting with potential tenants including:

If your housing is near a military base:
www.ahrn.com (Very active site for relocating military)
www.militarybyowner.com
www.gosection8.com (For recruiting Section 8 tenants)
www.rentals.com (For relocating families)

In addition to marketing on these web sites you should also utilize your social media connections. If you have a nice 3 bedroom home for rent, just give it a shout in Facebook, Twitter, or Linkedin with something like this:

"Nice 3 bedroom, 2 bath home for rent. Give me a shout if you know anyone looking for a great place to rent."

You can also post pictures to Facebook, Twitter, Linkedin, and Pinterest to share your message and get help from your social media connections in finding a tenant.

Signs: Signs are very effective and will get your phone to ring with potential tenants as well. Be sure to use a sign that is easy to see and easy to read.

Screening for the best tenants

Once you have successfully found some tenants who want to move into your nice home you must diligently qualify them prior to allowing them to move in. This qualification process starts with the rental application. I recommend using a thorough application and the first step to being a great tenant becomes their diligence in completing the entire application. If they only partially complete the application I generally will disregard them as a potential tenant. If the application is completely filled out we will then complete our screening of the tenant. We will verify employment and rental history first. We do this by asking for copies of their most recent pay-stubs and then calling their landlords. Both the employment verification and the landlord reference are great indicators of what you can expect from your future tenants. Provided all references and employment look good, we will then pull criminal background and credit. You then have a lot of information available on the potential tenant including employment, where they have lived and how long they have stayed, their criminal background, references and their credit history. With all the data you have collected you will be able to make an informed decision.

Being diligent with the rental application and screening process will provide you with a path to get great tenants into your property. Remember, the goal is to get the most qualified tenant who can fulfill your job description including paying rent on time and taking good care of your property.

Being a landlord can create nice income streams, build your long-term wealth, and provide substantial tax advantages. The challenge for most investors is the commitment to learn to become a great property manager so that your tenants pay rent on time and take good care of your houses. During a recent phone call I had with Michael Jake, he summarized property management success like this.

"Set a goal to become a great property manager and use the systems you establish."

It does sound simple, yet it is profound, that a key to making it easy is simply to learn and then establish and use your systems to make it effective. Michael and his wife manage a large portfolio of their own properties and I consider this to be great advice.

Today's real estate market is providing a great opportunity to buy the right houses at the right prices to make this a very nice income stream. In recent years, the rental market has strengthened as more people are renting now than in the past. Along with the increase in demand for nice housing has come the opportunity to get better quality tenants.

Buying houses with OPM (other people's money)

Even though housing prices have dropped so much, they still are an expensive purchase and investing in houses is still capital intensive. That is why you should also learn to buy houses without using any of your own money and without relying on bank mortgages.

In today's real estate market a good real estate investor should be able to find and acquire houses at a 40% discount price point. What that means is that the purchase price and all the necessary repairs together will not exceed sixty percent of the value of the house.

Here is an example:
Purchase price of house: $50,000

| Necessary repairs to house: | $10,000 |
| Value of house after repairs: | $100,000 |

The total investment is $60,000 and the house is worth $100,000 which equates to a 40 percent discount on the overall value. Looking at it the other way, the $60,000 investment has $40,000 of built in equity upon purchase of this property.

In my market here in Richmond, VA, a house like this one will be a typical 3 bedroom, 2 bath house in a county suburb working class neighborhood. This house in Richmond will rent for $900 per month creating a nice income stream for the joint venture investment. The primary on-going expenses associated with holding real estate are taxes and insurance. In Richmond, the taxes and insurance combined will be about $150 per month for the house in this example which leaves $750 net for the on-going monthly income stream for the joint venture.

The $60,000 investment has now been used to pick up $40,000 of gross equity and a $750 monthly income stream. I hope you are wondering how this gets applied back to the members of the joint venture because the answer is anyway that the Self-Directed IRA and Real Estate Catalyst come to terms. For simplicity sake, let's assume that the two joint venture members agree to a 50/50 split in this venture.

With a 50/50 split, the $750 monthly income stream is split so that both members receive $375 each month; along with this monthly dividend style income stream both member also will share the upside equity at some point in the future.

Let's make one last assumption to show how the ultimate return can be easily calculated for both members of this joint venture. Let's assume that both members hold onto this investment property for five years and then sell it for $100,000 which is today's value of the house. What did both members earn on this joint venture?

Self-directed IRA earnings:
$375 per month for 60 months:	$22,500
Upside equity split of the total $40,000:	$20,000
Total return over the five years:	$42,500
Total investment made:	$60,000
Annualized return on investment:	**14.16%**

Real Estate Catalyst
$375 per month for 60 months:	$22,500
Upside equity split of the total $40,000:	$20,000
Total return over the five years:	$42,500
Total investment made:	$0
Annualized return on investment:	**Infinite**

This is an example of a win-win transaction for an IRA that can joint venture with a sharp real estate catalyst. The real estate catalyst can invest without needing a traditional bank mortgage to buy real estate and will earn $42,500 which is an infinite return since he made no capital investment. The IRA invested $60,000 and received dividend type earnings of $42,500 which is an annualized return of 14.16%. Details of how to put together deals like this one are further explained in Chapter 8 "Be The Bank: Financing Income Streams."

CHAPTER 6 SUMMARY

1. What would your job description for tenants include?

2. Section 8 is a _____ subsidized program.

3. What is a web-site that you can use to find tenants?

4. A _____ application is the first step to screening a tenant.

5. Ask for the most recent _____ stubs to verify tenant employment.

Chapter 7

EINSTEIN'S INVESTING MODEL:
WHAT WOULD ALBERT DO?

My educational background in electrical engineering provided me with a lot of math and science courses. That is likely
the reason that I have always liked Albert Einstein. Einstein
was the German born physicist who is commonly known as
the Father of Modern Physics for his deep intellect. He provided society with great discoveries such as the theory of rela-
tivity, relationships between energy and mass, and so many
other physical truths that he earned a Nobel Prize in 1921.

How does Albert Einstein factor into a book about
cash flow? He was a mathematical genius, which led to
his contributions to modern finance. Einstein knew how
to create a passive cash flow through an understanding of
compound interest.

Albert Einstein is credited to providing us with three
great quotes regarding compound interest. I cannot personally attest to these quotes since I did not personally
hear him speak them and there is some controversy on
whether or not he did actual say them. Regardless, of the
origin, I do love these quotes that are often times credited
back to Einstein.

"The Most Powerful Force In The Universe is Compound Interest"

"The greatest invention of all time is compound interest"

"Compound interest is the 8th wonder of the world"

"Compound interest is the greatest mathematical discovery of all-time"

In case you forgot what compound interest is: **Compound interest** arises when the interest gets added to the principal, so that the interest that has been added *also itself* earns interest. This addition of interest to the principal is called *compounding interest*.

A retirement account, for example, may have its interest compounded every year: in this case, an account with a $100,000 initial principal and 20% interest per year would have a balance of $120,000 at the end of the first year, $144,000 at the end of the second year, and so on. Mathematically this is how it works:

$$FV = P(1 + r)^Y$$

FV = Future Value
P = Principal
r = Rate
Y = Years

If you have $100,000 (Principal), earn 8% (r) for 15 years (Y) you can mathematically calculate the future value with the formula as:

$$FV = \$100,000(1+.08)^{15}$$

After 15 years, the value will be $317,216.91 (assuming you compound interest annually). Understanding the end result of the future value is more important than understanding the mathematical equation involved.

Even though I am an engineer, I really do not like to have to manually compute future value using a mathematical formula and I am certain you don't either. The good news is that you do not need to compute it manually. There are many great resources you can use to calculate compound interest. I like the compound interest calculator at www.moneychimp.com as it is very easy, but there are many others available as well. I like to carry my compound interest calculator everywhere I go. I got this way because I believe Einstein's quotes of course; my preferred way to calculate compound interest is to use the app on my i-phone. I use the "Hopping Toad Software" app available in the i-tunes app store. Here is one more example of the power of compound interest for you to consider:

What happens with a low rate of return?

Starting Principal (P): $100,000
Rate (r) = 2%
Years (Y) = 20
Future Value (FV) = $148,594.74

What happens with a high rate of return?

Starting Principal (P): $100,000
Rate (r) = 12%
Years (Y) = 20
Future Value (FV) = $964,629.31

In this example, starting with $100,000 and investing for 20 years the difference between 2% and a 12% return is $816,034.57 That should capture your attention on the subject of compound interest and you should now be thinking about how you can get at least a 12% return on your investment.

A natural progression from compound interest calculations came the rule of 72. The rule of 72 is a simple method to determine how long it takes to double your money based on the rate of return. Numbers other than 72 could be used, but 72 is more easily dividable for most interest rates typically calculated.

As an initial example, lets say you start with a balance of $100,000 and can earn 2% in a CD or 8% in a real estate investment. What is the length of time for your $100,000 investment to double for each investment.

CD: 2% compounding interest: 72 / 2 = 36. This means it will take 36 years to grow your investment from $100,000 up to $200,000 if you earn 2% per year in a CD.

Real estate: 8% compounding interest: 72 / 8 = 9. This means it will take 9 years to grow your investment from a $100,000 balance up to $200,000 if you earn 8% in your real estate investment.

Millions of people are earning 2% or less in money-market accounts and CDs so it is important to know the return. Below is a table that will show you the value of earning a great return on your investment as indicated by the Rule of 72.

Rate of return	Years to double investment
2	36
4	18
6	12
8	9
10	7.2
12	6
14	5.1
16	4.5
18	4
20	3.6
22	3.3

There is a direct correlation between your invest-ment decisions, the returns you generate, and your long-term cash flow achieved. Albert Einstein provided us with numerous discoveries that forever altered society. I think if Albert was with us today he would be working on discover-ing the best way to get his money to work for him by earn-ing the greatest returns while managing the risk associated with his investment choices.

Albert Einstein would understand the long-term dif-ference between earning two percent in a CD investment and the potential to earn eight to fifteen percent invest-ing in real estate. Once you understand compound inter-est, and the impact your investment decisions will have, you will be ready to find the best investments to maxi-mize your returns while managing your risks. One of the biggest opportunities exists for the young people reading this book. Starting young and learning to invest will super-charge your long-term growth. Discovering the best invest-ment models will lead to a profound change in the balance of your accounts and your long-term wealth. The rule of 72 is easy to remember and an important way for you to easily get a feel for your return on investment. Everyone would love to see their funds double, and the higher the return, the faster they will double. Millions of people are settling for a very low return in a CD or have seen the balance in their 401k drop like a rock. Now is a great time to learn to invest your funds passively and with minimal risk into real estate so you can earn eight to fifteen percent returns on your investment.

CHAPTER 7 SUMMARY

1. Do you better understand the importance of compound interest?

2. If you start with a $100,000 balance, earn 2% per year for 20 years, what is your ending balance?

3. If you start with a $100,000 balance, earn 12% per year for 20 years, what is your ending balance?

4. If you earn 8% on your investment, how many years will it take for your total balance to double?

Chapter 8

Be The Bank: Financing Income Streams

Banks are a lot like every other business in the world. Every business sells a product or service and makes a profit for providing the product or service. The products and services that banks sell is simply money. They make money by providing loans, CD's, checking accounts and other financial products.

Essentially banks use their client's deposit accounts to enable them to make loans. If the bank has a client's $20,000 CD account it will be able to use those funds to fund loans such as this example below:

Mortgage: 4.5% APR
Credit Card: 14.9% APR
Student loans: 6.0% APR

They will likely be paying a two percent return on the CD account and then loaning against that deposit fund making between six and eighteen percent interest. To show exactly how this works would require a detailed analysis of the fractional reserve system. The bottom line is that banks make a lot of money by taking on deposit accounts and then loaning money out at specified interest rates to consumers all over the world.

The important concept is that lending money can create tremendous income streams for the institution or person that lends the money. If the financial institution is providing consumer credit in the form of credit cards they will also be charging a lot of fees. The fees include annual renewal fee's, late charges, over limit fees and so on.

The past few years lenders have tightened up their lending practices and that has led our economy into a credit crunch where small businesses and individuals have a much harder time getting the capital that they need in order to continue their operations and start up new businesses.

The good news is that real estate is on-sale all across the country; the bad news is that it is still a capital-intensive business. Even though you can buy investment real estate for less than the price of a new car; a new car still costs a lot of money. If you want to buy several houses per year to create your new income streams you will need to find a way to finance them. I advocate buying investment real estate without needing traditional bank mortgages. In order to do that the real estate investor needs to work with individuals who want to earn great returns and essentially be their bank.

There are two basic types of financing that can be structured to provide great returns for everyone involved.

1. **Debt financing** – This is typical bank style financing that includes an interest rate and points. Points are essentially another form of interest, but it is pre-paid. For example if a bank is loaning $100,000 on a mortgage and they charge two points. The two points equals

$2,000 and they collect that fee up-front when the loan is originated, rather than on a monthly basis.

2. **Equity financing** - An alternate form of financing that that does not include interest or points, instead the borrower pays the lender with a portion of the equity and dividends in the form of rental income.

Below are four different investment models that will further explain the income you can create by lending money on real estate transactions. These funds can be loaned out of an IRA or right out of your checkbook.

Investing Model One – 6% Return

Be the bank and earn a passive, steady income every month for many years. You can purchase a note or create a note for someone to purchase a house. For this example, lets loan $100,000 on a nice house and charge six percent interest for twenty years. This is similar to a bank providing a mortgage on a house, other than you will be charging a much higher rate of interest and amortizing the loan for twenty years rather than the traditional thirty years.

What is your income stream and return in this investment model one?

Loan structure: $100,000 at six percent for twenty years
Collateral: The house
Security: Deed of trust (mortgage) and promissory note will secure your interest in case of borrower default.

Monthly payment from borrower: $716.43
Total of 240 payments: $171,943.45

The cash flow income stream is $716.43 per month and it is created by loaning $100,000 on the purchase of a house. The total interest earned over the twenty years is $71,943.45 for this investment model. This is an example of a slow and steady income stream created by the loan provided.

Some keys to safely securing this income stream are the borrower and the collateral. If you are going to be the bank you will need to minimize your risk by qualifying both the borrower and the collateral (the house). The borrower should be providing you with a down payment so they have some "skin in the game." You will also want to check your borrowers credit history. To qualify the house, you will want to be sure to get a licensed appraiser to appraiser the value of the house. You will want to lend less than the house is actually worth. Finally, you will also want to have all of your documents prepared by a good attorney. These documents will secure your interest in the house, name you as the mortgagee on the insurance policy, and protect your interest with title insurance

Being the bank is a nice, passive income stream. You can minimize your risk by consulting with an attorney and covering all of your bases along the way. The remaining investing models are also passive ways for you to create income by being the bank. Each of them assumes you will properly minimize your risk in the same way as just presented.

Investing Model Two – 10% Return

Investing model one provides nice, slow and steady returns for twenty years. What if you want to increase your cash flow to ten percent? I am certain that the millions of people earning two percent in CD's right now would love to learn to earn a ten percent return.

Investing model two creates a ten percent return by providing short-term loans to real estate investors and simply charging ten percent interest. Who would be willing to pay ten percent interest? There are many real estate investors who are paying eight to twelve percent interest on short-term loans. These are loans that allow a real estate investor the opportunity to purchase a house, fix it up and flip it to a retail buyer. They use this strategy to create their own income stream, just like the one presented in Chapter 4 "Be the flipper: Flipping for large chunks of cash."

Investors need a solid source of short-term funding to create their income stream. For the remaining investment models I term the real estate investor as the "catalyst" and the person who is providing the loan as the investor. The catalyst does all of the work including finding the deal, negotiating, all the fix up and repairs. The investor who lends the funds creates a passive income stream.

The typical source that a catalyst uses for a short-term loan is a hard money lender. It is called hard money because it is hard for the catalyst in terms of expense. Many hard money lenders charge 12 – 16% interest and 3 – 8 points. A point equals one percent in interest. For example if a catalyst needs to be borrow $100,000 for six months from a hard money lender who charges fourteen percent interest and six points, his total financing charges will be:

$100,000 borrowed
14% interest only = $1,166.67 per month
6 Points: $6,000

Total charges over six months = $7,000 in total interest payments and an additional $6,000 in points.

Grand total of interest paid: $13,000

They also typically have a number of other junk type fee's that are imbedded into the loan. You can see why this short-term financing is called hard money. You can also see why folks looking to flip houses would be happy to pay eight to twelve percent interest each month.

This is why I advocate not using banks or hard money lenders, instead flippers should be seeking private lenders who will be happy to earn a great return.

Investing Model Two — Case Study

Purchase price of home: $70,000

Renovation expenses: $30,000

After repair value: $140,000

Loan to value: Roughly 70% = good collateral

Financing terms:

Interest only loan, six months at 10% interest only

Monthly payment: $833.33

Total payments over six months: $4,999.98

Investor profit on loan: $4,999.98 in 6 months

*** 10% passive return is the income stream ***

Long-term growth at ten percent compounding interest will grow the initial investment of $100,000 to $732,808.95 in twenty years

Investment model two PLUS -16%

Every time I stop in at a fast food restaurant they ask me if I would like to biggie size my combo. If you are creating cash flow and income streams by being the bank, you may want to do the same thing. If you like the sounds of a ten percent passive return making a short-term loan to a real estate catalyst why not go big and juice it up to a sixteen percent return?

This is a hybrid transaction between a hard money loan and the easy money loan I highlighted in investment model one. It is a little more painful for the catalyst and not every flipper will want or be able to pay this high of a return. Personally I like to lend on these terms, but when I am flipping houses I would not accept these terms. That being said, it is a lot cheaper for the catalyst than traditional hard money loans.

To biggie size this investment model simply add in three points. What does that do to the returns? It is like adding some rocket fuel to the equation. Using the same case study as the previous example and adding in the three points you will see the returns for the investor jump to sixteen percent.

Purchase price of home: $70,000
Renovation expenses: $30,000
After repair value: $140,000
Loan to value: Roughly 70% = good collateral
Financing terms for investment model two PLUS:
Interest only loan, six months at 10% interest only and three points
Monthly payment: $833.33
Total payments over six months: $4,999.98
Three points: $3,000
Investor profit on loan: $4,999.98 in six payments and $3,000 in points charged for a total of $7,999.98.
*** 16% passive return is the income stream ***
Long-term growth at 16% compounding interest will grow the initial investment of $100,000 to $2,401,930.49 in twenty years

Did you catch the long-term difference between ten percent and sixteen percent returns? Adding in the three points will create an additional $2,401,930.49 over a twenty-year period of investments. That should reinforce the importance of the chapter on Albert Einstein and compound interest. If you lend out of your Roth

Self-directed IRA you can do this tax-free. Investing for retirement in a self-directed Roth IRA is the ultimate way to create tax-free cash flow for retirement and for future generations!

The first two investment models create nice cash flows for the person lending the money and still allow the real estate flipper/catalyst to earn enough to make it work for everyone involved. Each of these first two investment models are based on a traditional debt financing structure. Another form of financing is equity participation based. Instead of structuring a traditional loan with points, interest, and amortization periods you can structure the loan using a joint venture and share the equity.

With this equity participation model the catalyst again does all of the work including finding the deal, negotiating, construction and renovations, and so on. The funding comes from the investor/lender who is essentially passive, does no work but provides all the money for the transaction. Equity participation financing with a joint-venture can work well for both the catalyst looking to flip houses and for the long-term lender type catalyst as presented in chapter six "Be the landlord: Rental income streams."

Investment model three – 32% equity participation

Type of investment: Short-term investment equity participation.

Returns: Based on up-side equity and there are no payments, no interest, and no points charge.

Investing Model three – Case Study

This is a three-bedroom home purchased in Richmond, VA with the intent of flipping. It was purchased using 50/50 equity participation meaning that the flipper/catalyst and the investor/lender will split the upside profit 50/50.

Purchase price: $72,000
Renovation expenses: $32,000
Home sold for: $145,000 (six months)
Total profit (taking out closing costs): $34,000
Equity split: $17,000 for flipper and $17,000 for investor
Annualized return for investor: 32.6% return!
Long-term: $104,000 investment, 32.6% return, 20 years will lead to over $37,000,000!

If you can learn to work with a flipper willing to share his equity 50/50 and make some excellent investments you could learn to create a 32% return. I am sure that caught your attention when I showed the twenty-year growth was over $37,000,000.

Does that sound too good to be true? I usually think anything that sounds too good to be true, must be too good to be true. However, there are some really good flippers who are willing to share their equity. These flippers can provide tremendous returns to the investor/lender. If you could make some great returns inside a Self-directed Roth IRA these earning could be used tax-free. Allow yourself to imagine creating an income stream to produce $37,000,000 over twenty years tax-free!

In order to create consistent returns over thirty percent each year, the investor/lender will need to become active instead of passive. He will need to find multiple flippers and catalysts to keep his money active and consistently purchasing the right houses to generate these types of returns. The critical component of equity participation becomes the flipper/catalyst.

Investment model four – Long term, Passive Growth

Investment model four provides long-term growth with steady, passive returns using a joint-venture approach with equity participation on rental properties. It is a joint venture between the catalyst and the private lender.

As always, the catalyst does all the work including finding the house, construction, and all the property management. The private lender provides all of the funding and does no physical work. This investment model has the potential to yield in the ten to eighteen percent range.

Investing Model Four – Case Study

Three Bedroom ranch style home we invested in using investment model four in Richmond, VA.

This home was purchased using 50/50 equity participation meaning that the landlord/catalyst and the investor/private lender will split net rental income and the upside profit 50/50.

Purchase price: $46,000
Renovation expenses: $34,000
Total investment: $80,000
Home rented for: $900 per month
Taxes and insurance expense: $150 per month
Net rental income stream: $750 per month
Income stream split 50/50: $375 per month to private
    lender and the catalyst/landlord also gets $375 per
    month.

Value of home today: $125,000 (for this case study we assume we sell in 5 years at today's value)

Upside equity split 50/50 when sold: $22,500 for Investor / private lender and $22,500 for catalyst/ landlord

Total cash return in five years: $22,500 in rental income and $22,500 in upside equity = $45,000

Annualized return for investor: 11.25% return

Long-term: $80,000 investment, 11.25% return, 20 years will lead to over $674,668.42

Each of these four investment models provide tremendous cash flow for everyone involved. The real estate catalyst gets the opportunity to actively invest and take advantage of today's market and the private lender/investor has the opportunity to make fantastic returns becoming a bank.

CHAPTER 8 SUMMARY

1. Name the two types of financing that can be structured?

    1. _____

    2. _____

2. Investing model two creates a ten percent return by providing _____ loans to real estate investors.

3. Investment model two plus adds in _____ along with interest to create a larger return for the investor.

4. Investment model four is designed to provide _____ growth for the investor.

Chapter 9

Recycle, Re-use, and Re-purpose

Along the way of creating income streams centered around real estate and financing transactions you will find additional small streams that are also presented to you. One of them that I like to embrace involves the process of reusing materials and items found inside of houses. I am not a tree-hugging environmentalist, but I do drive a hybrid and I do believe each of us should do our part for future generations by recycling.

We all know that the petroleum industry has been making tons of money the past several years, but did you know that investing in real estate can put you into the oil business? Many houses we work on have old oil heating systems that include abandoned oil tanks. We get rid of the oil heating systems and typically go with a new heat pump. We always had someone come pick up the left-over oil tank to get rid of it until we realized that often times there is still oil left in the tank. Once we realized there was oil left in the tanks we began giving the oil away to families in need. We have given away tons of oil. If you have an oil tank and want to capitalize on it, you can easily sell the extra oil by placing a simple ad on Craigslist. The title should read "1/2 off oil" and in the posting just note that they need to come to your house and pump it themselves to receive the big discount. You will be surprised how many people want your oil for half price and you can often get them to remove the existing tank as well.

While working on houses we literally throw away many tons of debris every year. This past year I began to encourage the contractors on our team to recycle their metal materials.

Recycling just one aluminum can save enough energy to run a television for 3 days and that is a fact few people talk about. There is no limit to the amount of times that aluminum can be recycled. If not recycled, aluminum will last another 500 years before decomposing. A good friend of mine, Bill Stratton, owns a metal recycling business here in Richmond. His metal recycling business allows many of our materials from old houses to be reprocessed and recycled.

The fact is that the United States is the number one trash producing country in the world. Mount Rumpke in Ohio is a mountain of trash that has become a local landmark complete with guided bus tours. Aluminum metal contained in houses, that can be recycled, includes aluminum siding, gutters, window frames, and chain linked fencing. Demand for aluminum is high due to the high strength to weight ratio that it provides.

The recycling process consists of re-melting the metal, which consumes about 95% less energy than manufacturing brand new aluminum.

Besides aluminum there are often times a lot of copper that can be recycled during renovation. Copper comes from old plumbing, wiring, and heat pump condenser units. Copper is an expensive metal and is the reason you should always lock your crawl space and attempt to secure your heat pump condensers. We have had a few encounters with the copper bandits stealing our copper this year and it is very expensive to replace it.

All metals can be recycled and you will create an income stream while recycling the metal. You will be surprised how much extra money you can generate just by recycling metals. What I often do is encourage our subcontractors to recycle the metal and I let them keep the proceeds as a bonus for doing it. They are happy to recycle knowing it puts some extra money into their pockets.

If you do not want to take the time to recycle, you can often just re-sell items such as appliances. They are easy to sell on Craigslist. We have sold many stoves, refrigerators, dishwashers, washers, and dryers. You can sometimes sell other items as well. If you don't want to recycle your materials and you do not want to resell them, another other option is to give them away. I have done this with big bulky items such as piano's. I just post an ad that says first people who come to remove my piano from my house can have it free of charge. You will be surprised what people will come haul away when it is free. You can also donate many of your old appliances, doors, windows and building materials to your local Habitat For Humanity. They will be able to sell them in their RE-store and I highly recommend giving them away to this fantastic organization!

When rehabbing houses you are likely to encounter houses with a lot of stuff left behind from the former owners. Sometimes when negotiating the lowest price possible I will tell the owners to take what they want and leave the rest. Some owners do not have the resources and energy required to properly empty and clean out their homes.

American Pickers is a great show that features two guys, Mike Wolfe and Frank Fritz, who travel across the country searching for treasures in other people's trash. These two guys can be seen on the History Channel scouring through others stuff in hopes of finding a great prize in the form of anything they can make a buck on. In order for them to find that elusive prize they absolutely have to know exactly what they are looking for, be able to quickly evaluate the condition and determine the value so they can make an offer that will provide them with something they can make some money on. I do not watch very much television, but if you are buying houses you should check this show out so you begin to learn what to watch for when clearing out other people's trash as you may someday get lucky and find a treasure. If you buy a house with a lot of vintage items that appear to be in great shape you might want to contact a picker or just take a shot at it yourself. You may be able to sell them on eBay or to a local antique store or pawn shop.

You can check out Frank and Mike's websites and get a feel for the kind of items they are currently looking for. Their list typically includes old games, movie posters, pedal cars, bicycles, and much more. I currently have my eye on some items in a house I am working on buying. These items include an old catcher's mitt, a motorcycle, a bicycle, and some old tennis rackets. I am trying to negotiate these items as part of my purchase of the home.

There are quite a few similarities in picking and buying houses directly from the owners. Frank and Mike are excellent at quickly establishing a rapport with their sellers and gaining trust. When you meet to buy a house direct from an owner, you will also need to be able to quickly establish trust. One more thing you will learn while watching this show is how to negotiate. Both Frank and Mike are excellent negotiators and Frank loves to make an offer that any reasonable buyer can't refuse and he is a master at bundling items together to get the best possible deals. Watch how they negotiate and you will be able to learn how to improve your negotiating skills as well.

Here are the links to their websites:

Frank Fitz: www.frankfritzfinds.com
Mike Wolfe: www.antiquearcheaology.com

I have not personally found anything really collectible or valuable in any of the houses I have bought. I have however found some old stuff along the way including items like old typewriters, old tools, and other miscellaneous vintage items. However in the summer of 2011 I did find three boxes of comic books in the attic of a house we were working on in Glen Allen, VA.

My brother David is always buying, selling and collecting items including comics, baseball cards, coins, pez, and old toys so I just check with him to see if a potential collectible has any value. He quickly determined most of the comics were from the 1980's and not worth very much money to a collector, however, they would be nearly priceless to my nephew Cameron. I thought it was a great idea to give these three boxes of comics to Cameron and my brother agreed to come pick them up the next morning. Later that night David called me and had a special request directly from Cameron that they not wait until the next morning to come collect his comics. They came and picked up the comics and I tell you it was like Christmas in July! Cameron was so excited to get these comics and I loved giving them to him. He went straight home and started looking through them and reading them that night.

Below is a picture of Cameron and the comics that we gave him. The value of these comics to Cameron is priceless and we loved watching him light up like a Christmas tree when he got them!

Chapter 10

Creating Cash-Flow With Subject-to Mortgages (Bonus)

By Michael Jake

If you are ready to buy some properties but do not wish to get new financing such as mortgages from a traditional bank you have some options. You can joint venture, buy with seller financing, or buy the house subject to the existing mortgage remaining in place after closing.

How would you like to buy houses without needing to get a new mortgage? Buying houses subject-to means that the buyer makes the acquisition without paying off the existing mortgage on the property. The ownership of the property changes to the new owner, but the debt does not get formally assumed and does not get paid off at closing. The mortgage remains in the name of the person who originally took the loan when the house was originally purchased.

People ask me, why in the world would a seller convey the ownership of their house but leave the existing mortgage in their name for the new seller? It usually comes down to eliminating their payment and providing them with mortgage relief. They are highly motivated sellers who need a solution to their situation. Selling their house subject-to is a means to that end. They typically do not have a lot of equity in the property and need to sell fast.

Many people who are able to sell their house subject-to are moving soon or they used their home as a rental and the house is about to become vacant. Often times the owner can't afford to make payments on an empty house without it being a financial hardship. Monthly payment relief is the main reason why they're selling us that house. Basically they are willing to take the risk for us to make their payments going forward even though they're the ones financially liable for the loan. Usually what happens is their credit starts improving because we are making their payments on their loan on time.

Usually the owner deeds their house over to you, but it is not a loan assumption, as the mortgage remains in the name of the seller. We should be clear that there is a clause in the mortgage that states selling subject-to is a violation of what they call the "Due on sales" clause inside the mortgage. This due-on sales clause says that if they transfer the property that the bank or lender has the right, not the obligation, to call the entire balance due.

Subject-to investment strategies work well for our investing model because we will not buy a house subject-to without being completely certain that the incoming rental rate will fully support the existing, underlying monthly payment. We buy with that as the primary criteria. Beyond the monthly commitment we are looking for loans that have been amortizing for a period of time and with low interest rates established. We buy subject-to with the goal of buying and holding for the purpose of acquiring assets that provide positive monthly cash flow.

The process of buying subject-to is not risky for the real estate investor, but can be risky for the seller if the real estate investor is not able to make payments in the future. It is very important that the investor understand the risk that his buyer is incurring and be certain that payments can always be made on behalf of the seller. Buying subject-to the existing mortgage remaining in place works well for the investor as it allows control of an asset without having to go get a new mortgage from a bank. Buying houses without needing a bank mortgage can save thousands in closing costs on each transaction. It also provides the real estate investor financing at low interest rates and loans that have been amortizing for a while. Buying houses subject-to allows the real estate investor to buy as many houses as they desire to meet their investing goals for cash flow and net worth.

My subject-to investing model is primarily looking for sellers who have become accidental landlords or have to move out of town. The sellers typically have existing mortgage balances between $130,000 and $250,000 and with loans that were originated between five and six years ago with low interest rates in place. We like the subject-to investing model as it allows us to get control of a house with very little capital extended, rent it out for positive monthly cash flow and then look for a pay-day on our equity at a future date.

The typical house we are purchasing subject-to will have a mortgage balance of about $200,000 with a low interest rate and have a total monthly mortgage payment of around $1,100. In our market here in Colorado Springs, this home will rent for $1,300 - $1,395 per month. That will provide us with positive monthly cash flow that is created with as little of our own money used as possible. We will look to sell this same home in the future for around $225,000 leaving a future payday of $25,000.

When we rent out this same home we use our lease to own program that will have the new tenant/buyer put down a 3.5% deposit up-front which is typically around $6,000. The subject-to investing model then provides cash flow in a variety of methods including:

1. Up-front: Payment from new tenant/buyer of $6,000
2. Monthly: Monthly positive cash flow of $200 - $300 per month
3. Future: When home is sold, cash from equity of about $25,000

The seller gets out of a property where they didn't want to be in that situation and avoids being an accidental landlord. They also get monthly payment relief as they no longer have to make their own mortgage payments. The real estate investor gets to control a nice asset without needing to obtain a new bank mortgage and will enjoy future cash flow from three different methods noted above.

Afterword — Now What?

Congratulations! Now you have some new tools in your toolbox to help you create income streams. I am a capitalist and a conservative risk taker. I have used these tools successfully to build substantial positive cash flow. The good news is that real estate is on sale, widely available, and provides fantastic opportunities in every market.

This book has presented several different income streams. Some are active streams meaning they require work. These streams include wholesaling houses and flipping houses. With these income streams you have the opportunity to create income but they require quite a bit of work. Wholesaling allows you to create an income stream without risk and without much cash. The wholesaling income stream can provide a steady set of paydays. The key to wholesaling is making deals and getting in the middle of as many deals as you can. You need to find your own houses, build a strong buyers list and then connect the dots to put deals together. Wholesaling is an easy way to jump into real estate and quickly earn your first payday. Flipping houses requires you to learn your local market values, find and manage contractors, and build a team. Generally speaking there are more moving parts and things that have to go just right to reap the reward. Flipping houses creates larger buckets of cash flow but the timeline is often three to five months to get your payday.

I have committed myself to being a lifetime learner. The key to creating income streams starts with investing in yourself. I love learning new things and getting outside my comfort zone. What is your driving force for creating income streams? Is it to pay down your debt, pay off a car, save for college tuition, or prepare for retirement. Remember, everyone has money problems. Some have too much money and are fearful of how to invest it and others do not have enough money and cannot make their financial commitments. One of the best things I get to enjoy is spending a lot of time with my family. My wife and children have all been involved in our real estate business and I have been blessed to spend so much time with them.

One of the greatest objects that will challenge your success is FEAR. I understand the fear factor associated with real estate given the challenges associated with today's marketplace. This fear can be overcome as you invest in yourself by gaining knowledge.

Some of the income streams presented are passive meaning they require very little work. These are the perfect income streams for long-term wealth building and monthly income streams. The drop in overall real estate values has created new opportunities for collecting real estate assets and renting them out. The rental market has strengthened in recent years and it is not hard to find good tenants in today's market.

If you are fortunate enough to have plenty of money available but have the challenge of how to invest it, you are in position for passive returns on investment. You can joint venture with a strong real estate catalyst and create outstanding returns by being the bank. With the right catalyst you should be able to create returns of eight to twenty percent investing today. This is the reason I get excited calculating compound interest. If you are one of the millions of people with declining 401k or IRA values, now is the time for action. Consider rolling your retirement funds into a self-directed IRA and take control of your investing future to creating the returns to get your retirement back on-track.

In order to further facilitate the investment in yourself I highly recommend that you take the following steps:

1. **Read:** Take time to read as much as possible. Set a goal of reading every day of your life. I have provided tons of reading material in the blog section of www.investing-nownetwork.com. Sign up for my newsletter to receive timely market information on a regular basis and also receive my free special report.

   If that is not possible in your current situation ask your-self what can change to make it happen because it is that important to continually read. Maybe you need to get out of bed a little earlier, stay off of social media, or turn the television off. Maybe you can listen to books while you are driving in your car. Find a way to make it happen and com-mit to reading to invest in yourself and increase your finan-cial literacy and cash flow knowledge.

2. **Network**: There are a multitude of places to network with like-minded people including local real estate in-vestor clubs, cpa meet-ups and more. You can find plen-ty of them right on meetup.com. Did you know that your income and net worth is generally the average of the ten people you spend the most time with? Take a minute and write down the names of the ten people you spend the most time with right now in the space below.

After reviewing the list do you agree with the assumption in the statement above? In the beginning of this book I shared that I want to always give back and help others in need so I am not suggesting that you only spend time with highly successful people. Personally I love the contribution of people like Mother Theresa who gave her life to the people of Calcutta. I am suggesting you begin to network with people who have a strong financial literacy and create a network of financial friends. These are friends who you will learn a lot from and who you can begin to structure joint venture deals with and mutually benefit one another financially. Networking with the right people is a key to your long-term success.

Finally I want to connect with you and hear your stories. What are your fears and challenges in today's market. What is working well for you? Tell me your success stories and how you have overcome your fears.

I invite you to connect with me using the following sources:

www.investingnownetwork.com

This is the website that I have created specifically for investors. Please stop by and join my newsletter so that we can stay in touch. You will also have the opportunity to check out my blog and get insider tips on all of the income streams presented in this book. I have also included my speaking and training schedules.

www.facebook.com/investingnow

Please take three seconds, stop by our page to "LIKE" us. When you "LIKE" this page you will have the opportunity to download my free special report. Facebook will allow you to stay connected as I provide tips, tricks, and specials, Most importantly it is a vehicle that will allow us to connect right on the wall. Stop by the wall and introduce yourself, share your story and interact directly with me.

3. **Coaching**: Behind every great team, in sports, business, or Hollywood is a great coach. I am a big fan of all sports and I love watching great coaches get the most out of their teams and lead them to championships. This year we saw the New York Giants win the Super Bowl over the favored New England Patriots. The Giants had just nine wins in the regular season, but they have a great Coach in Tom Coughlin. Their coach rallied the team for a fantastic play-off run that led to a Super Bowl victory.

    Last year, Virginia Commonwealth University made an unbelievable run through the NCAA tournament. VCU did not necessarily have the best, biggest, or fastest players in the NCAA tournament. What they did have though was Coach Shaka Smart. It was Coach Smart who knew how to get the most out of every single player, focus the energy, and put together wins that led all the way to the final four!

    Cash Flow Now has provided information on how to create multiple streams of income. If you are a reader who wants additional help putting together the remaining pieces in wholesaling, flipping houses, building a rental portfolio, or being the bank, I have good news for you. We have coaching programs at all levels that will help systematize and automate each of these income streams. Many good players become great players with additional coaching. Our coaching programs can help you take the next steps in your quest to create income streams. If this is something that interests you, please check out the "Coaching" page on www.investingnownetwork.com.

Can you help me with one favor? Please take a moment and leave me a review on Amazon, or Barnesandnobles.com. I greatly appreciate all reviews!

I had great feedback from my first book *Investing Now*. I look forward to continuing our discussion on *Cash Flow Now* and interacting with you as you embark on your journey to find new income streams.

All My Best To You!

Jim Ingersoll

Jim Ingersoll

Author, Entrepreneur, and Coach

www.investingnownetwork.com

Meet the Author

Jim Ingersoll is a successful Author, Entrepreneur and Coach. He has bought and sold hundreds of houses and is a licensed Class A Contractor. His educational background includes an undergraduate degree in Electrical Engineering and a graduate degree in Engineering Management. Jim loves investing in creative real estate, speaking, and coaching others. He has two daughters, Melisa and Carisa and has been married to Cheryl for 25 years.

Glossary

Amortization: a loan payment plan that allows debt to be paid gradually in the form of monthly payments.

Appraisal: a professional appraiser's opinion on the value of a property. The appraiser provides a written estimate of a property's fair market value based on the sales of comparable homes in the area and the features of the property being appraised.

Appreciation: an increase in the value of real estate property.

As-is condition: the purchase or sale of a property with no repairs completed.

Assets: items of value, such as real estate.

Blog: a "web log" that contains commentary on events or general topics.

Buyers market: a slow real estate market where the buyers tend to have the advantage.

Cash flow: net operating income minus the total of all debt and expenses.

Code violations: a housing infraction that makes a structure unsafe, condemned, or in violation of local building codes.

Compound interest: Interest paid on principal balance and on the accrued and unpaid interest of a given loan.

Condemnation: a process where a public authority will require the owner to fix the property prior to allowing anyone to enter and use the property.

Consideration: typically in the form of an earnest money deposit, but can be anything that has value, and legalizes a contract.

Contractor: an individual or company who contracts to work on your home for renovations or trade services.

Creative financing: any financing arrangement that does not involve traditional bank financing.

Craigslist: a popular website in which users sell a variety of goods or services.

Debtor: the person or entity that borrows money.

Deed: a document that legally transfers ownership of property from one person or entity to another. The deed is recorded at the local courthouse.

Deposit (earnest money): money paid by the buyer to ratify a sales contract when purchasing real estate.

Eviction: A legal process to remove a tenant from a rental property.

Hard money loan: a loan based on the condition and value of the property as the primary criteria in the approval process. It is applied toward the purchase of the property upon settlement.

Entrepreneur: a person who creates, builds, and establishes his own business.

Equity: an owner's financial interest in a property; it is the difference between current value of the property and amount owed on the property.

Equity financing: a form of financing that has no stated interest rate; rather the return is based on the upside equity when the asset is sold and the monthly income streams.

Fannie Mae: Federal National Mortgage Association (FNMA); a federal enterprise owned by private stock holders that purchases residential mortgages and converts them into securities for sale to investors.

FHA: Federal Housing Administration that assists home buyers by providing mortgage insurance to lenders.

Home inspection: an examination of the structure, systems, and all aspects of a home.

Landlord: A real estate owner who chooses to rent his property to a another party, known as a tenant.

Multiple Listing Service (MLS): a marketing database established by cooperating brokers. It is a listing service that compiles information on properties for sale.

Offer: buyers' intent to purchase a home at a specific price and time.

OPM: the process of using other peoples money to buy real estate

PITI: Principal, Interest, Taxes, and Insurance: the four elements of a monthly payment that compose the complete mortgage payment for a borrower.

Points: a point is equal to one percent of the principal amount of your mortgage. For example, if you get a mortgage for $125,000, one point means you pay $1,250 to the lender.

Private lending: a form of lending that eliminates the need for traditional bank financing.

Property tax: a tax charged by local government that is used to fund municipal services.

Real estate: land and all structures permanently attached to the land.

Sellers market: A hot real estate market, with low inventory levels in which sellers have the advantage.

Tenant: A person or entity who chooses to rent or lease a property from a landlord.

44035776R00084

Made in the USA
Middletown, DE
02 May 2019